Parakeets

2nd Edition

by Nikki Moustaki

Parakeets For Dummies®, 2nd Edition

Published by: **John Wiley & Sons, Inc.**, 111 River Street, Hoboken, NJ 07030-5774, www.wiley.com

Copyright © 2021 by John Wiley & Sons, Inc., Hoboken, New Jersey

Published simultaneously in Canada

For general information on our other products and services, please contact our Customer Care Department within the U.S. at 877-762-2974, outside the U.S. at 317-572-3993, or fax 317-572-4002. For technical support, please visit https://hub.wiley.com/community/support/dummies.

Wiley publishes in a variety of print and electronic formats and by print-on-demand. Some material included with standard print versions of this book may not be included in e-books or in print-on-demand. If this book refers to media such as a CD or DVD that is not included in the version you purchased, you may download this material at http://booksupport.wiley.com. For more information about Wiley products, visit www.wiley.com.

Library of Congress Control Number: 2021939750

ISBN 978-1-119-75524-1 (pbk); ISBN 978-1-119-75529-6 (ebk); ISBN 978-1-119-75530-2 (ebk)

Manufactured in the United States of America

SKY10027409_060421

Contents at a Glance

Table of Contents

Introduction

Many people remember having a parakeet when they were a kid, and many kids (and plenty of adults!) today either have one, want one, or will receive one as a gift. As a companion, the parakeet has it all. It's little enough for even the smallest apartment, is as affectionate as any lapdog, and can out talk even the largest of parrots. What more could you ask for?

About This Book

Parakeets For Dummies is for people interested in parakeets — whether you want to know about parakeets before you acquire one, you have recently brought a parakeet (or two) into your home, you're a parent buying this book your child, or you're a young person buying it for yourself. Maybe you want to discover the essential scoop on getting your new bird set up properly, as well as general care information. Perhaps you simply need a refresher on the best way to take care of your feathered companion or want to understand it better and start some advanced training. Perhaps you're ready for a new bird but aren't sure if a parakeet is right for you and your family. If any of the above describes you, then you've come to the right place.

As you read, keep an eye out for text in *italics*, which indicates a new term and a nearby definition — no need to spend time hunting through a glossary. And monofont points out Web addresses for additional information worth checking out. You'll also run into a few sidebars (the occasional gray box); although the information in the sidebars is good, it's not essential to the discussion at hand, so skip 'em if you want to.

Foolish Assumptions

In writing *Parakeets For Dummies*, I made some assumptions about my readers:

>> You're one of the millions of people who wants a parakeet or who has a family member who wants one (or more) and you've come to this book to learn about their care and training.

>> You already have a parakeet, or two, or twenty, and you want to brush up on parakeet care and learn a few things that you don't already know.

>> Maybe you're a volunteer at a parrot shelter or rescue and you want to be able to educate your adopters more thoroughly.

>> Perhaps you want to begin breeding these popular little birds and want some information on how to make that process go smoothly.

Whatever the case, whether you're a newbie or a seasoned parakeet guardian, there's something in this book for you.

Icons Used in This Book

While reading *Parakeets For Dummies*, be on the lookout for these icons, sprinkled here and there:

This icon flags tips and tricks that will help you be the best parakeet pal you can be.

This icon points out information that's so important you'll want to be sure to remember it.

This icon highlights information on things that could harm you or your parakeet.

TECHNICAL STUFF

This icon flags information that you can use to impress your friends with your amazing bird knowledge, but it isn't absolutely necessary, so don't feel the need to memorize it.

Beyond the Book

You can find a little more parakeet-related on `https://www.dummies.com/`, where you can peruse this book's Cheat Sheet. To get this handy resource, go to the website and type *Parakeets For Dummies Cheat Sheet* in the Search box.

Where to Go from Here

Parakeets For Dummies is a reference, so you don't have to read it in order from start to finish. Begin with Chapter 4 if you need basic set-up information, flip to Chapter 7 if you're trying to learn parakeet-ese, or head to Chapter 2 if you're still undecided about adding a parakeet to your family. (Although if you prefer to start at the beginning and read until you reach the back cover, you're welcome to do so.)

1
Introducing the Parakeet

Chapter **1**

Parakeets: More Than Just Pretty, Whistling Birds

The word *parakeet* is a generic term for any smallish, slender bird in the parrot family that has a long, tapered tail. But when most people think "parakeet," they think of the small, brightly colored bird common to most pet shops and to almost everyone's childhood.

Parakeets are about 7 inches in length (with the English budgie at around 9 inches), and most of that length is taken up by the tail. This species, *Melopsittacus undulatus*, also called the *budgerigar* (*budgie* is its nickname), is found in large flocks in the grasslands of the Australian outback. The English budgie has the same Latin species name, even though it is much larger.

WHERE PARAKEETS COME FROM

Parakeets arrived in Europe around 1838, brought from Australia by British naturalist John Gould and his brother-in-law, Charles Coxen, who raised the first *clutch* (batch of babies). Europeans found that these birds were easy to breed, and wealthy people fell in love with them. They soon became popular in Germany, Belgium, France, and Holland.

A yellow mutation occurred in Belgium around 1875, leading to other color mutations, including olive, dark green, gray-green. Companion parakeets were simply green, as they are in the wild, until around 1881 when a Dutch bird keeper found a blue chick hatched in the nest boxes. This blue bird was responsible for other mutations: cobalt, mauve, slate, gray, and violet.

The parakeet arrived in America around the late 1920s, but didn't become popular as a companion until the 1950s. Today, there are hundreds of color mutations and variations. Even so, the most common colors are the most popular: green, blue, yellow, and white.

The American Parakeet versus the English Budgie

Though the American parakeet and the English budgie both got their start in Australia, the American parakeet is more similar to its wild cousin than the English budgie. The English budgie is what hobbyists call an *exhibition bird* or a *show budgie,* because it is often shown in large budgie shows (kind of like dog shows, but for birds). It's nearly twice the size of the American parakeet, and it claims its English name because the British, who received the exhibition size budgie from Western Europe, sent the exhibition budgie to America.

The English budgie is basically *domesticated*, which means that it has been changed from its wild form using selective breeding practices. This kind of selective breeding (choosing to breed only the animals that have desired traits so that the young will also have and pass on these traits to future generations) is what humans have done with dogs for thousands of years. (Notice how different dog breeds look so dissimilar from one another — it's hard to imagine that they all originated from a couple of species of wild dog.) Though no parrot is truly domesticated, the English budgie is the closest.

Though technically called the budgie, the terms *parakeet* and *budgie* are interchangeable (see Figure 1-1). Some people call the larger version of the parakeet the budgie and the smaller version the parakeet — but it really doesn't matter which term you use. For the purposes of this book, I refer to these little birds as parakeets. The basic differences are as follows:

>> **Size difference:** The American parakeet is smaller, thinner, and more streamlined than its British counterpart. The English show budgie is stately looking, with a full, prominent chest and forehead. Its eyes are barely evident and its beak is tucked into the feathers of its face. It is 8½ to 9½ inches long, whereas the American is about 7 inches long.

FIGURE 1-1: The English budgie (left, male) and American parakeets (right, female, male).

>> **Temperament:** The American parakeet is feistier than the English budgie and may be more active than its mellower cousin. Both birds are good companions. Whichever type you choose, you can tame the bird into a wonderful pal, or keep a pair to watch and add some liveliness to your home.

>> **Lifespan:** Lifespan is one of the primary differences between the parakeet and the budgie. The big English budgie lives about 7 to 8 years, and the American parakeet can live 14 years or more with the proper care.

The Anatomy of a Parakeet

Knowing your bird's anatomy will help you describe a problem to an avian veterinarian if you ever have to do so. You can also speak like an expert with other hobbyists. Here are the primary parts of your parakeet (see Figure 1-2):

>> **Crown:** The crown is the top of the head.

>> **Nares (nostrils):** The nares are at the top of the beak.

>> **Cere:** The *cere* is the fleshy area above the beak that contains the nostrils. It becomes blue in mature male parakeets, and brown in breeding condition females. When parakeets are young, it's white to light pink. The cere is a purplish-pink in males and a whitish-blue in females (when females are not in breeding condition).

>> **Beak:** The upper and lower *mandibles* (jaws) make up the parakeet's beak. The parakeet is classified as a *hookbill*, meaning that the beak is shaped like a hook and is perfect for cracking seeds and breaking twigs.

>> **Ear:** Your parakeet has small flat holes for ears, and they're covered by thin feathers that protect the ear. This is why you can't see them unless your bird is wet.

>> **Eyes:** The parakeet's eyes are on either side of its head so that its field of vision is about 300 degrees. By contrast, a human's field of vision is about 120 degrees. This wider

view of the world is because the parakeet is a prey animal and needs to be constantly on alert for predators. Parakeets, like many birds, have a third eyelid called a *nictitating membrane,* which is a thin, semitransparent lid that washes the eye like a squeegee and closes for protection.

>> **Throat:** The throat is just beneath the beak and extends to the breast.

>> **Nape:** The nape is the back of the neck.

>> **Shoulder:** The shoulder is at the top of the wing nearest the parakeet's back.

>> **Breast:** The breast is just below the throat.

>> **Foot:** Everything that most of us think of as a bird's leg is actually a bird's foot. That's why the "knee" appears to bend the wrong way — it's actually the bird's heel. The parakeet's foot is *zygodactyl,* meaning it has two toes in front and two in back, perfect for grasping and climbing.

>> **Vent:** The vent is where your bird eliminates. In a human, this would be a combined anus and urethra. Birds' urine is not separate from their droppings; urine is combined with the fecal portion of the dropping as a small wet outer ring.

>> **Primary feathers:** Parakeets have ten long primary wing feathers that aid in flight.

>> **Secondary feathers:** The secondary feathers on the wing occur after the primaries, closer to the body.

>> **Rump:** The rump is beneath the primary flight feathers on the parakeet's lower back.

>> **Mantle:** The mantle is the back area between the shoulders of the parakeet.

>> **Crop:** The crop is a sac-like organ that's kind of like a "first stomach." It's where the food goes immediately after being swallowed and is located at the top of the breast.

>> **Syrinx:** The syrinx is equivalent to vocal chords in humans. It allows parakeets to talk and vocalize when air is pushed through it.

FIGURE 1-2:
All the parts of a healthy parakeet.

Chapter **2**

Is a Parakeet Your Perfect Companion?

I f you're trying to decide whether to bring a parakeet into your home, you've come to the right chapter. Even if you already have a parakeet, this chapter has something for you too. Here you'll figure out what to expect from a parakeet (from its bubbly personality to the dreaded messes it makes) and what your parakeet expects from you. I walk you through the challenges posed by children and companion animals (whether birds or cats or dogs). I also give you information on keeping more than one parakeet.

Knowing What to Expect from a Parakeet

As wonderful as they are, parakeets are still considered wild animals, just as are all companion parrots. Though parakeets are about as close as a bird comes to being domesticated (other than the canary), they still have their quirks. Knowing what to expect from your parakeet — from personality to lifespan — will make your relationship with your bird better and stronger.

A great personality

As with humans, each parakeet is an individual with its own individual personality. Some are sweet and affectionate, while others may always remain fearful or aggressive. What you receive from your parakeet depends a lot on what you put into it. In general, a kind, careful guardian can tame a parakeet into a loving companion.

If you buy two parakeets that look similar, you may worry that you'll never be able to tell them apart. After you get to know them, you'll see that they have personalities of their own, likes and dislikes, different mannerisms, and different aptitudes for talking and training.

Noise and talking ability

If you require an absolutely quiet home, then parakeets are not the bird for you. You're never going to prevent noise. They chatter, sing, and even talk for a good part of the day, though they do have their quiet moments. Fortunately, parakeets aren't loud, but they are persistently noisy. Just as beauty is in the eye of the beholder, loudness is in the ear of the hearer. Some people aren't bothered at all by parakeet noise, while others may be annoyed by the constant chirruping.

A healthy and happy parakeet is quite noisy. Beware the silent bird — it may not be feeling well. Birds tend to hide signs of illness very well, so being quieter than usual is definitely cause for concern.

Parakeets are excellent talkers. They can even out-talk some of the larger bird species. Parakeets can learn hundreds of words and phrases and say them clearly and interchangeably. *Cocks* (male birds) are more apt to talk earlier and more frequently, but *hens* (female birds) have been known to do their share of chatting as well.

Companionship

One of the best reasons to get a parakeet is for companionship. Parakeets are affectionate companions and bond readily to any human who is patient and kind. Your parakeet may love to stand on your shoulder while you do your chores or watch television. He'll preen your eyebrows and sing into your ear.

TIP

If you want your parakeet to be an affectionate companion, devoted to you, keep just one, as long as you're able to pay a lot of attention to it. If you have less time to spend with a single bird, consider a pair. A pair of parakeets will keep themselves entertained and occupied, and you won't have to worry about your bird being home alone and pining for you.

Mess and more mess

Birds are messy. You'll definitely be walking on a crunchy floor, and perhaps even a bit of water to go with it after the parakeet has taken its bath. You may even find seeds growing out of your carpet (yes, it has happened to me)!

TIP

Acrylic cages do the best job of keeping mess at bay (more about this in Chapter 4). However, even if you buy all the seed-catching devices and all the hooded cups on the market, you're not going to prevent mess. Get used to it and love your bird all the more for being the imperfect creature that it is.

A decade or more of life — if you take care of the bird

Unfortunately, most parakeets only live a few years in the average home due to improper care and feeding, neglect, and accidents. But with the proper care, a parakeet can live 12 to 15 years.

The larger English budgie, because of its specific breeding, tends to live to be only about 7 or 8 — and that's an old English budgie. They may be able to live longer with exceptional care.

Knowing What Your Parakeet Expects from You

Your parakeet relies on you for all of its needs: proper housing, nutrition, playtime out of the cage, and safety. You're responsible for every aspect of its life. In the following sections, I let you know what your parakeet needs from you, but here's a short list of the basic things your parakeet needs:

>> **A clean cage:** You'll need to clean the bottom of your parakeet's cage nearly every day, or your bird's waste will become crusty and turn into a fine dust, which your parakeet (and you) can inhale. This is not healthy. Once a week, clean the cage and the surrounding area more thoroughly. (More on how to clean the cage in Chapter 9.)

>> **Water:** Offer your parakeet fresh water twice a day if you can; at least once a day for sure. If the water dish isn't empty (it shouldn't be anyway), throw out the remainder of the dirty water and replace it so that your parakeet always has a fresh water supply.

>> **Food:** Provide and change fresh and cooked foods once a day. Just as with water, if your parakeet hasn't eaten all the fresh or cooked foods you gave your bird the day before, throw out the old food and replace it with new. Uncooked foods like seeds or pellets can remain in the dish and you can just top them off. (*Note:* You should change the water twice a day if possible, but you need to change the food only once a day.)

>> **Playtime:** Your parakeet needs safe playtime out of the cage every day unless the bird is in a large flight cage at least three to four feet in length, or a larger aviary. Be sure to keep a close eye on your bird — and on your other pets — whenever your parakeet is out of its cage. Also, check your bird's cage and toys daily for wear and tear.

>> **Attention to his health:** Your parakeet can't just fly out to the vet's office when it feels a little under the weather. You need to watch your bird closely for signs of illness and take it to the veterinarian if you suspect something is wrong or if your bird has an accident.

>> **Empathy:** Your parakeet is relying on you for a hundred percent of its care and its recreational activities. Keep in mind that your parakeet is a bird of boundless space that must live in cage in a human home. Be sensitive to this and give your parakeet enough outside time on your shoulder, in a closed room or a safe area of the house, or offer a large flight cage or aviary.

>> **A safe home:** When you bring a parakeet into your home, you need to make sure it's a safe place for your bird to live. (See Chapter 4 for more information on parakeet-proofing your home.) Also make sure that your parakeet's housing is away from drafts and that the room where it lives doesn't get too cold or too warm.

In addition to these basics of bird care, your parakeet needs other things from you, covered in the following sections.

A good home

Parakeets need as large of a cage as your space and budget can afford. If you can't buy a large cage, then save up until you can. A cramped parakeet will be quite unhappy.

A parakeet's environment needs good lighting. It can be indirect natural lighting with some direct sunlight during the day (though the bird should always have half the cage in a shady spot where it can retreat in order to avoid sunstroke). Or, you can use special bird lamps, which you can get at the pet shop or online. A clip-on lamp and a full-spectrum bulb meant for birds should keep your parakeet healthy.

Ideally, the temperature in your parakeet's environment should be between 68° F and 72° F (20° C and 22.22° C). Make sure that your bird doesn't get too cold or too warm, and that it has clean, fresh water at all times in hot weather. You can tell if your bird is too cold if it sits with its feathers fluffed up; if it is too hot, it will open its wings at the shoulder joint and pant with an open beak. If your home is below 68° F (20° C) at night, make sure to cover the cage to keep in the heat and keep out drafts. (Chapter 4 offers some advice on how to keep your bird warm in the cooler months.)

TIP

Before bringing your parakeet home, make a space for his cage in an area where he's bound to get the most attention. I like to place my companion birds' cages in an area where they can see me most of the time, like in a family room or living room. They get the added bonus of being able to watch television (and believe me, they like it!). Your parakeet is *unlikely* to get a lot of attention in a garage, child's room, or patio.

Time

Expect to spend at least two hours a day with your bird. Spend more time with your parakeet on the days when you have more time — but two hours is the bare minimum. That's a commitment of at least 14 hours a week, possibly more.

Cleaning, feeding, watering, and playing with your parakeet all take time. You'll also spend time making arrangements for it when you go away on vacation and you'll spend some time in the veterinarian's office as well.

WARNING

If you're thinking, "Oh, she's exaggerating — I'll be able to take care of my parakeet in fewer hours than that," you may want to ask yourself why you want the bird in the first place. Spending time with your parakeet — even doing the not-so-fun things like cage cleaning — should be something you enjoy. If you're looking for ways to avoid it, perhaps a bird isn't for you.

Routine

In the wild, parakeets schedule their day around the sun. They understand the seasons and how to behave when water or food is scarce or plentiful. In nature, the same events happen day after day, year after year, and these birds are programmed to go with the flow.

TIP

Create a daily routine and try to stick with it. Your bird should know exactly when you're going to feed him, when you're going to clean his cage, when he's coming out for playtime, and when it's time for bed. If you keep a routine with your parakeet, it will eventually alert *you* when you've missed a step. If your life is hectic, just do the best you can. The good news is that parakeets aren't as fussy about a daily routine as some of the larger parrots.

Deciding Whether a Parakeet Is Right for You

If you're still not sure whether a parakeet is right for you, thinking about who you're getting the bird for (yourself or someone else, like your son or daughter), how much money you'll need to spend taking care of the bird, and what kind of home you can provide is a good place to start. Parakeets bring joy and happiness into millions of homes, and your bird can bring the same to yours if you've thought seriously about what you'll need to give.

VACATIONING WITHOUT YOUR BIRD

Some people don't think about things like vacations when they buy an animal. Try to recruit a responsible friend, neighbor, or loved one who will take care of your parakeet when you're away. If you can't find anyone, call your local avian veterinarian and inquire about boarding there.

If you're away from home more often than you're there, you may want to think twice about getting a parakeet. Parakeets are great companions — which means that they like your companionship as much as you like theirs.

Looking at why you're getting the bird

If you're an adult and you want a parakeet for yourself, you're off to a good start. Parakeets are not just for children, and they're not starter birds. Parakeets and adults can have a wonderful relationship, as can parakeets and children.

Here are some good reasons to buy a parakeet:

>> You've always wanted a parakeet.

>> You've had your eye on a particular parakeet in the pet shop and you've fallen in love with him.

>> Your child wants a parakeet very badly and you (the parent) are willing to assume full responsibility of the bird.

>> You had parakeets as a child, you loved them, and you want to have one again.

WARNING

Some not-so-good reasons to buy a parakeet include the following:

>> You need something to match the drapes.

>> You want a bird and a parakeet is all you can afford.

>> You want a pet that's not going to live very long for your child.

>> Your cat ate the last one you had.

>> Your other parakeet died of a disease (you didn't take it to the veterinarian) and you need a replacement bird.

WARNING

If you're buying a parakeet for a child, realize that *you* will likely be the one who ends up taking care of the bird, even if the child promises to feed the bird and water it and clean the cage and play with it and love it every day. Though your child may have the best of intentions, more often than not, the parent assumes responsibility for the animal. (See Figure 2-1.)

Parakeets *can* provide a child with a sense of responsibility, compassion, and companionship. The qualities that a child learns from caring for a bird are qualities that he or she will use for a lifetime. Children who have parakeets learn to love, care for, respect, and maintain another being — and that valuable hands-on lesson lasts well into adulthood. Having a parakeet will also teach the important lesson everyone has to learn eventually — that nothing lives forever.

FIGURE 2-1: Children and parakeets can be good friends, but they must be supervised.

TIP

Even if the parakeet is the child's bird, place the cage in a room where the bird will get attention from the whole family. Explain to the child that the bird will be lonely in the child's bedroom because she is away most of the day. If the child is old enough, gentle, and handles the bird respectfully, you can allow her to play with the bird in her room. Problem solved. (See Chapter 6 for more information on helping your children to handle a parakeet safely.)

Knowing how much keeping a parakeet will cost

All the parakeet accessories that you'll need to get started, like a proper cage, cups, toys, and a play-gym, can take a chunk out of your wallet. A parakeet can cost anywhere from $10 to $25 for an

American parakeet, or $45 to $100 or more for an English budgie.

Then there are trips to the avian veterinarian for well-bird check-ups, which you should do yearly. When your avian veterinarian gets to know your bird, he or she will be better able to take care of it in the event of an accident or illness.

Parakeets cost around $15 per month in food and accessories. You may want to splurge now and then on extra toys or treats, which will bring the total expense higher.

Considering your other family members

If you're thinking about bringing a parakeet into your home, you owe it to the parakeet and the current residents — whether animals or humans — to think about how everyone will (or won't) get along.

Parakeets should not be allowed around babies. Parakeets often carry diseases that are communicable to people with under-developed or compromised immune systems, which include babies. Though toddlers have a stronger immunity, they may not understand that they have to be gentle with such a fragile bird.

Even kids that are a little bit older can harm the bird when the parent isn't looking. The child can let the bird out of the cage, try to catch it, or feed it something harmful. When you get a parakeet for a child (or have a child in the home), make sure that the child is mature enough to understand this animal's needs, and be sure to supervise your child's contact with the bird.

TIP

When you find the perfect spot for your new bird's housing, use brightly colored tape to mark a square around it on the floor with a few feet of space between the tape and the cage. Make a rule for your child that he or she must not ever cross the tape. This should help keep little hands out of the cage.

WARNING

THE "PITY" PURCHASE

Sometimes buying a bird that looks very ill is tempting. Perhaps he's the most plucked, sorriest looking parakeet of the bunch. The bird looks like it's going to keel over any second. You know the bird I'm talking about — the one who's hearing the angels singing already.

This bird is not only going to cost you a fortune in veterinary bills, it may infect your other birds with whatever illness it has, and the pet store is just going to buy another sorry bird to put in his place. You're always better off sticking with healthy birds from the beginning. Of course, if you know what you're getting into from the beginning by helping a sick parakeet, by all means do it, just be very careful.

If you feel really sorry for the parakeets in a particular pet store, you aren't obligated to go into that pet store anymore — and for goodness' sake, don't buy birds there. You can call your local Humane Society and hope that something gets done about the conditions in the store. You may want to call the store's owner as well — that usually works for a time.

One, Two — or More: Increasing Your Parakeet Population

If you want a sweet parakeet that lives for seeing you come home every day, a parakeet who is so enamored with you that you can barely move without it stuck to you like a burr, you'll want to have one — and only one — parakeet. If you get a pair of parakeets, they may want to interact only with each other, seeing you as an intrusion in their birdy love.

On the other hand, if you lead a busy life and you're not home for many hours of the day, you may want to consider getting a pair.

Just because you have a pair, or more, does not mean that your parakeets will not become hand-tamed or won't love you, but you may have to work a little harder to get them to see you as one of the gang.

A single parakeet, especially a single male, is more likely to talk. This doesn't mean that birds in a pair won't ever talk; it just means that the likelihood of getting them to talk is lessened the more parakeets you have.

Can you have three or more parakeets in a cage? If they are all males, you have a better chance that they will get along. Although female parakeets are more likely to argue and squabble, three females can live together too if they are all housed in a very large cage, flight, or aviary at the same time. If you have a true pair, a bonded male and a female, you don't want to add another bird unless you have a very large flight cage at least six feet in length to allow a pursued "rival" adequate space to escape, or else the existing pair may become territorial and can severely injure the "intruder," or worse.

Two parakeets interacting can be really cute if they like each other. They will sit together and preen each other. The male will do a little mating dance, strutting up and down the perch, rapidly tapping his beak against the perch or a shiny object. They will chitter-chatter to each other. These behaviors are all ways in which parakeets communicate.

When parakeets don't like each other, one may chase the other around the cage, not allowing the less assertive bird near the food and water dishes. One may begin to pull at the other one's tail feathers, which will suddenly appear curled at the tip, and fight more aggressively, even drawing blood. These parakeets should be separated into two different cages and closely supervised whenever exercising outside the cage, or else let out of their cages at separate times.

LOOKING A GIFT PARAKEET IN THE BEAK

Giving a parakeet as a gift isn't a great idea unless you have discussed it with the recipient and the gift isn't a surprise. You may think that you're giving a *parakeet,* but what you're really giving is a 12-year or more responsibility with a bird that the person may not like — and vice versa. Take into consideration that the person may have wanted to choose the parakeet on his own. Maybe you got him a blue parakeet and he wanted a yellow one. A gift certificate to a pet shop is a better option if the recipient has indicated that they really want a parakeet.

Remember: Holidays are the worst time to give a live animal to anyone. Holidays are traditionally busy times with lots of bustle and activity, and the poor parakeet may get lost in the shuffle. The holidays are a good time to buy bird books (such as this one!) and a gift certificate for a parakeet and the accessories that go with it.

Unlike some other species, parakeets rarely kill one another, but it can happen, especially if there are competing egg-laying females in housing that's too small. Parakeets who don't get along that are housed in too small of a space can also turn deadly. A new parakeet added to a cage or aviary with existing birds can also become a victim. You have to watch your birds very carefully in these situations and have separate housing ready in case of an issue.

Chapter **3**

Finding and Selecting a Parakeet

inding the "perfect" parakeet may seem easy — just go to the pet shop and pick one out, right? Well, that's one method, but doing a little homework may help you make a more informed decision about where and how to acquire your new friend. If you've already gotten your parakeet by pointing into a cage and saying, "Just give me one," you're not alone. I'll admit now that the last two parakeets I bought were from a pet shop, just little faces in the crowd, and they were wonderful. They're hard to resist, aren't they?

Choosing a Parakeet: Exploring Your Options

You can find many "kinds" of parakeets — young, older, tamed, untamed, different colors, and previously owned parakeets, just to name a few. Which parakeet is right for you depends upon what you want or expect from the bird. In the following sections, I cover the main decisions you'll need to make before choosing your perfect parakeet.

English budgie or American parakeet

The American parakeet and the English budgie are basically the same animal, except for size. The English budgie is more than twice the size of the American parakeet. It also has a shorter lifespan (about 7 years or so, as opposed to the American parakeet's 12 years or more), and its temperament can be a bit mellower than its smaller cousin.

If you want a hands-on companion, you'll find little difference in quality between the two birds, except that the English budgie may be a little easier to tame. Budgies are a little more difficult to breed, though, and can be at least four times more expensive than the American version. The English budgie can also be gentler than the American parakeet, even when not tame, and is usually less likely to bite. They may also be a little quieter in general.

Fledgling or adult

A *fledgling* is a young bird that has just come out of the nest and is able to eat on its own. This is the best time to get a parakeet if you want it to be hand-tame. Most baby parakeets are eating well on their own at 6 to 8 weeks of age and can be taken to a new home then.

An adult bird that has already been tamed makes a great companion as well. Parakeets reach young adulthood at 6 to 9 months of age. If you get an adult that has never been handled by humans before, you'll have to spend more time taming the bird.

TIP

If you want a really tame and sweet baby, try to find a breeder who will hand-feed a baby for you. The breeder will take the baby away from the parents while the bird is still reliant on them, and take over the parental duties. A bird who has been hand-fed as a baby will become very tame and comfortable with humans, because he'll be used to being handled. Or, if sold right from the nest between 38–42 days of age, they immediately become finger-tame quite easily.

TIP

So how do you know how old a bird is? You can tell the age of a parakeet in three ways:

>> **Leg band:** Most breeders put identification bands of the legs of their nestlings — the laws in many states require any birds sold to be banded. The band will have the breeder's ID engraved on it, as well as the state, the year hatched, and a number unique to your particular bird.

Keep in mind that you may have to remove the leg band if your bird seems annoyed by it. The band can also get caught on something and injure your bird's leg. *Never, ever* cut the band off yourself. Your avian veterinarian has a special tool to remove the band safely.

>> **Barring on the head:** In the normal varieties, baby parakeets have barring on the head (see Figure 3-1) and adults do not. The stripes disappear and are replaced by a solid color as the bird gets older. However, rarer color varieties may not be born with any head barring.

>> **The cere:** The *cere* is the patch of flesh just above the beak and is blue in adult males and pink or brown in adult females. The cere is whitish/pinkish/bluish in babies, with the male youngsters having a light purple cere, signifying that the parakeet is still young. The cere will change to its adult coloring when the bird is about a year of age. Breeding adult females will have a tan or deep brown cere.

Blue or green or . . .

Parakeets come in hundreds of colors and patterns. Even so, you'll probably only find a few colors (for example, white, blue, violet, yellow, pied, and gray) in your local pet shop, and the bird's color has absolutely no effect on the quality of the bird. No one color will make a better companion — simply choose the color you like the most. There is some anecdotal evidence that the normal green (wild color) parakeet might be a little hardier than some of the mutations. See Chapter 10 for more info on parakeet genetics.

FIGURE 3-1: A young parakeet still has barring on the top of its head and the beak is tipped in black, which will eventually fade.

Male or female

If you're buying your parakeet as a baby, you won't know its gender. No matter — just choose the one that you like. Males and females make equally good companions. Males tend to be more docile and females a little feistier when they reach maturity, but this isn't always the case, especially if the bird is getting a lot of hands-on attention. Males tend to be a little friendlier and social, whereas females can be more assertive and possibly a bit louder.

Both males and females can learn hundreds of words and phrases. This doesn't mean that your parakeet will definitely learn to talk. Like everything else, this is based on the individual personality of the bird and the dedication of you, the instructor, to provide lessens consistently. In general, males tend to be the better talkers.

WARNING

A female parakeet may lay eggs without a male around (or with a male around, and the eggs may be fertile in that case), which means that she may also become egg-bound, an emergency situation where an egg is unable to be passed (see Chapter 9 for information about egg binding).

Finding a Parakeet

After you've decided which traits you're looking for in a parakeet, you have to go out and find it. Fortunately, you have a variety of options — so if one place doesn't have what you're looking for, you can try another.

Pet shops

The concern with the *average* general pet shop is that the employees are busy with so many different animals and so many different dry-good products that they may not know a heck of a lot about birds (such as where the parakeets came from and how to recognize a sick bird when they see one). So before you buy a bird in a pet shop, pay close attention to the store itself, as well as to the store's employees.

TIP

When you first walk into the pet store, ask yourself the following questions about the store:

>> **Is the pet shop clean?** If not, get out of there right away.

>> **Do the birds have clean water?** If the water looks like Mississippi mud, not only should you leave; you should tell the store manager before you do so.

>> **Do the birds have food?** Again, tell the manager if they don't.

>> **Do the parakeets have enough room?** Overcrowding is a stressful situation for birds — you're better off finding a store that doesn't cram its livestock. If the birds have hardly any perch space and they're scrambling all over each other, the cage probably doesn't offer enough room.

>> **Do the birds look healthy?** If you see any parakeets sleeping on the floor of the cage, looking kind of puffy, that's a warning sign that the birds are sick. Leave these birds alone.

>> **Does the staff know what a parakeet is?** If you ask for a parakeet and the salesperson starts to put a canary in a box for you, that's not a good sign.

>> **Is the staff helpful and friendly?** Don't bother with a store that has hostile or uninterested sales staff — they won't be helpful if you have a problem with your bird after you get it home.

If you answer "no" to any of these questions, move on and find another pet store — one where every answer is a "yes."

If you are lucky enough to have a bird-specific store in your area, one that only sells birds and bird supplies, that store is worth the gas money it will take to get there, even if it's a little out of your way. The employees in that store will likely know more about birds and about what you need. They also may know where your parakeet came from and may know more details about it.

TIP

Whether you buy from a general pet shop or a birds-only store, ask some questions about your potential parakeet before you consider taking it home:

>> **Where do you get your parakeets?** If the employee doesn't know, reconsider buying from that store. Some bird-only stores may purchase from small breeders who handle or hand-feed their parakeets.

>> **Does this parakeet come with a health guarantee?** If the salesperson says, "What's that?" run fast and far away from there. (See the nearby sidebar on health guarantees.)

>> **What is this parakeet eating?** "I dunno," is a terrible answer. "Seeds, what else would it eat?" is equally poor. If the answer is that all the birds are fed seeds/pellets plus fruits and vegetables and other fresh foods, you're likely to be happier with a bird from that store. Of course, the

parakeets aren't typically as well cared for in stores as are the larger birds, so don't leave a bird you've fallen in love with there simply because the employees don't know much about it.

>> **How old is this parakeet?** The store employees should be certain of the bird's age. *Remember:* For the fastest taming results, you'll want a young bird.

As with anything else, *buyer beware.* If you buy a bird without a health guarantee and your parakeet keels over, you're stuck with a dead parakeet and no recourse. Most good stores allow you a certain amount of time to take your bird for a checkup and will take the bird back if there's a problem. If you have no health guarantee, then you're buying the bird at your own risk.

The swap meet or flea market

You can often find parakeets sold at your local swap meet or flea market, but be aware that if you buy a parakeet from a swap meet, you may not be able to find the person who sold it to you the very next week. Try to get a business card or a phone number when you purchase your bird so that you have someone to call if something goes wrong.

Online classifieds

Sometimes breeders advertise in online classifieds. The breeder may have just a few pairs and some babies to sell. This may be a good choice because you may get to see where your bird came from and may even make a friend out of the seller, a person who can help you if you have trouble with your parakeet. Many small breeders also handle or handfeed their babies, making them much tamer from the beginning.

You can also find "secondhand" parakeets online from someone who no longer wants their birds. Most of the time you'll have to pay a re-homing fee, but the bird will sometimes come with a cage and accessories.

Parakeet breeders

You can find a breeder online or through your local bird club. If you're very lucky, you'll find a parakeet breeder who breeds for fun, or English budgie *breeder,* someone who breeds for mutations and for showing. This person can even become a mentor to you, helping you become more knowledgeable in the hobby, and help if you decide to breed your own birds someday.

When you arrive at the breeder's home, look for cleanliness and check to see if the birds are being treated humanely. Do they have enough space? Do they have fresh, clean water? Is the temperature too warm or too cold? If you feel comfortable with the conditions of the birds, then you should be comfortable purchasing a bird from this person.

Ask for a health guarantee and the right to return your parakeet or budgie should it not get a clean bill of health from your avian veterinarian.

Bird rescue

Many birds in rescues all over the country are looking for a new home. Birds end up in rescue for a variety of reasons. Sometimes the previous owner can no longer care for the bird or is unable to take it to a new home during a move. Sometimes the bird is given up due to an allergy or change in life circumstances. A second-hand bird does not necessarily have anything wrong with it, and by adopting one you should not feel like you're getting a "lower quality" bird. When you adopt a bird from a rescue, not only are you helping a bird gain a new home, you are opening up a cage in the rescue for another bird that needs placement.

Do a Google search to find a bird rescue in your area. Often bird rescues do not have a centralized location, but rely on fosters to care for their birds while they are waiting for homes. Fostering a parakeet before you adopt is a great way to find out if a parakeet is the best bird for your lifestyle.

Bird shows

Bird shows are a great place to meet breeders and enthusiasts and to learn more about parakeets and budgies. A bird show is a great place to meet people and to see all kinds of different colored parakeets and variations in English budgies. Your local bird club will probably hold a yearly show.

TIP

Walk around the show and talk to people. Take down some phone numbers and emails and make some friends. These people know the most about your parakeet and can help and advise you with any situation you may encounter.

Searching for a Healthy Parakeet

When you've decided on the color, age, gender, and type of parakeet you want, and you've decided where you're going to buy the bird, you have to go about choosing a healthy one. Choosing a healthy bird is actually easier than you may think.

TIP

When you buy your parakeet, you should make a well-bird checkup appointment with an avian veterinarian, just to make sure the bird is as healthy as it looks.

You'll need to be on the lookout for several traits when you're shopping for a healthy parakeet:

>> **Eyes:** A healthy parakeet's eyes are round, clear, and bright. You shouldn't see any crust or discharge from the eyes. The eyes should seem alert, as if the bird is ready for anything.

>> **Nose and nares:** A parakeet's nostrils are called *nares* and they're located on the *cere,* which is the fleshy part just above the beak. The nares should be clean and without discharge. The cere should not be crusty or peeling. (A budgie with a crusty brown cere is an adult female in breeding condition.)

>> **Feathers:** The feathers of a healthy parakeet are shiny and tight, lying flat against the body. A parakeet with excessively ruffled feathers may be ill. Feathers should cover the whole body — if you notice bald patches, the parakeet has a problem. The only acceptable reason for a parakeet to have patches of feathers missing is if his or her mate (or other parakeets in the store's cage) is pulling them out. Birds with shabby feathers may also simply be suffering from having too small of a cage.

>> **Feet:** A parakeet should have two feet (preferably, though some do fine with one) and the feet should be clean and free of debris. Missing toes are fine. It happens. The parakeet should be able to perch easily on both feet. Sometimes, a parakeet chick can have splayed legs or other foot problems, but this is no reason to turn it away. A parakeet with leg and foot issues still has its wings and will be able to get around if allowed full flight in a large cage (*full flight* means that the bird's wing feathers aren't clipped).

>> **Vent:** The *vent* is at the base of the tail beneath the bird and is the place where waste is eliminated and where eggs are laid. The vent should be clean, not crusted with feces or other material.

>> **Attitude:** A healthy parakeet is active and chattery, always on the move. A parakeet who is sitting on the bottom of the cage, fluffed and sleepy, may be having a health problem. Try to choose a parakeet who is wandering around the cage socializing, eating, and bathing. This bird may be healthier than Mr. Sleepy in the corner of the cage, trying to get away from the others. If a particular parakeet in a cage full of birds is being chased relentlessly and picked on, that bird might be ill. Tell the manager of the store and ask them to remove the bird to an isolated cage.

Chapter **4**

Home Tweet Home: Preparing for Your Parakeet

fter you've chosen a parakeet, you have to choose the type of housing where your bird will thrive. Buying a cage and just sticking the new bird in it with whatever paltry accessories were included is like buying a house but not furnishing it. Your parakeet needs more than a couple of perches to make a proper parakeet pad, and this chapter helps you choose the right ones, and shows you how to set up your cage in a way that will be pleasing to Polly.

Your Parakeet's Home

Having Polly flying around the house 24 hours a day isn't safe or practical. Parakeets aren't as destructive as some other parrots, but they can get into mischief inside an average home, which could end very badly — not to mention that you'll find parakeet droppings all over the place. Your parakeet needs its own place to rest, eat, and play. Although birds aren't really meant to be caged (a wild bird would shudder at the thought), a cage or aviary is the most practical piece of equipment that you and your bird will own.

Size is everything

The old saying "bigger is better" refers to many things (boats and burritos, for example!), but the cliché works for bird cages, too. When you're looking for a cage for your parakeet, look for the largest cage that the space in your home and your budget will allow.

When you go to the pet store, you'll find some cages labeled as parakeet cages, and you may be tempted to trust the label. These are usually small, pastel-colored cages geared toward being kept in a child's room. This kind of cage is an unacceptable home for your parakeet unless you are just using it as a sleeping cage or a cage you will place outdoors (with supervision) to give your bird some sunshine and fresh air.

The minimum cage size for one parakeet or a pair is 24 inches long, 20 inches high, and 18 inches wide (give or take a few inches). For more than two parakeets, the cage should be at least 36 inches long, 30 inches high, and 20 inches wide (again, give or take). Remember, this is the *bare minimum*. Your parakeet will use and appreciate more space.

WARNING

If you purchase a large cage, be certain that the bars of the cage are not wide enough for your parakeet to stick its head through and become injured, or even die, as it struggles to pull its head free. Cages labeled for cockatiels are fine and will be larger than a cage typically marketed for parakeets.

Flight cage, aviary, bird room, and habitat

A *flight cage* is one that, in theory, gives your birds space to fly, although smaller cages are sometimes marketed as flight cages.

A flight cage is usually free-standing, may be on wheels (which makes moving and cleaning it easier), and may have multiple doors. Look for a flight cage that is at least 48 inches long, the minimum length your bird will need to actually use its wings and not just go from perch to perch using its wings to assist in hopping.

An *aviary* is a larger cage, usually built outside, although you can purchase or build an indoor aviary as well. An aviary is typically large enough for you to walk inside and has space enough for multiple birds to fly around. Parakeets do very well in aviaries because they are sociable birds that tend to get along. They can even be housed with cockatiels, other types of docile, small-beaked keets, and even canaries and finches, if the aviary is large enough.

A *bird room* is a room in your home that you dedicate to your birds. It should be fully bird-proofed (see later in this chapter for bird-proofing details) and functions like an indoor aviary. Each bird or pair or amiable group should have their own cages where they can eat, bathe, and sleep. Every morning, you can open the cage doors and allow your birds some freedom. At night, the birds will most often return to their cages by themselves and you can close the doors again. Only birds that get along should be allowed out at the same time.

A *habitat* is the ultimate bird housing. You'll often find bird habitats in zoos, but you can create a smaller version in your yard to give your birds the most natural experience possible. A habitat is usually larger than an aviary and has some natural elements included, like a water feature, trees, branches, and a sandy or gravel floor.

WARNING

If you do decide to build an aviary or habitat, make sure that it has a double door for entry and exit. This is a door that you open and then close behind you, leaving you in a small, cage-like space. Then you can open the second door to the aviary. This prevents your birds from escaping as you come and go from their housing. Also, any outdoor cage must have double wire to prevent predators from getting to your birds. An outside layer of wire is built over the inside layer, like a cage inside a cage.

Looking at shape

Square or rectangular cages are far better than round ones. Your parakeet will like a corner to bunch himself into when he's scared or sleepy, and a round cage doesn't offer that comfort. Square or rectangular cages also offer more cage space for the same basic cage size. For flying, a cage should be longer than it is wide or tall.

Considering cage materials

Most typical cages are made of metal and plastic, and some are powder-coated to add color or texture. Metal cages are preferable to wooden cages, which are often sold for finches. Although wooden cages are attractive, your parakeet will certainly begin to destroy it in no time.

WARNING

Be careful that the coating on the bars or mesh is nontoxic and won't harm your birds. If you notice that your parakeet is picking away at the coating, *remove it from the cage immediately* and get a new cage that doesn't have coating on the bars. Ingestion of this coating can be deadly.

TIP

Cages made entirely or partially of acrylic (a type of plastic) eliminate a lot of mess. These cages can be more expensive than the standard metal cages, but they're attractive, safe, and can save you time cleaning. Some even come with mechanical ventilation that cleans the air inside the cage — a nice feature for those who suffer from allergies. The downside is that acrylic cages lack bars, and the bars allow for climbing, which is a favorite pastime of a caged parakeet. Adding climbing toys and swings will make up for that.

Keeping safety in mind

You'd hope that all bird cages were safe, but unfortunately, that's not the case. When you're in the market for a cage for your parakeet, make sure that you choose one that will keep your bird safe and healthy.

TIP

Many cages have guillotine-style doors that can snap down onto a little feathered head and break a neck. These doors open from the bottom when you push them up and are quite weighty. You're better off finding a cage with doors that open from the side, like the door to a house, or that open from the top and pull down, like a drawbridge. (See Figure 4-1.) If you have a cage with the guillotine-style doors, invest in inexpensive quick link clips from the hardware store. These links will prevent a potential escape artist from having its little feathered neck clamped in a heavy door.

FIGURE 4-1: Cages with drawbridge style doors are safer than guillotine style doors.

Ideally, your cage should have a grating on the bottom to keep the bird away from its own mess. You can line the tray beneath the grating with newspaper, which has a disinfecting effect from the ink and makes it easy to see the droppings (you'll want to check your bird's droppings when you clean the cage for any abnormalities, which can be an indication of illness). Because parakeets are ground feeders, if you don't have a grate keeping the bird from the paper, the newspaper ink will stain a light-colored bird. You can purchase blank newsprint paper in this case.

There are also pre-cut cage liners made for some cage sizes. If you like this idea but can't find the right size, simply cut paper to the size of your tray and then pull out the soiled paper once a day or so, leaving the clean paper underneath.

Bird litter, typically made from walnut shells, corn cob, or recycled newspaper, is also a popular cage substrate, and this is fine to use, too, but people tend to clean the cage less when they use litter because seeing the mess is more difficult. *Remember:* If you use bird litter, you should still clean the cage at least every other day.

WARNING

Using litter may pose other dangers as well. The litter can become moist, allowing fungus and bacteria to grow, which can be deadly to your bird. Also, if the bedding is within reach of the bird, it can ingest the substance and may become ill, even die. In addition, never, ever use cedar shavings near any bird. These shavings may smell nice, but the fumes from cedar can cause respiratory distress. Don't use kitty litter either — it's too dusty and dangerous if ingested.

Deciding where to put your bird's cage

Your parakeet will be most comfortable placed close to a wall or in a corner, so that only two of the four sides of the cage are facing the great wide open. The wall(s) will afford your parakeet the feeling of safety. A cage that's hung from a chain or placed out in the open may cause your parakeet to become nervous and frightened. Hanging a cage poses two issues. First, if you are hanging a cage, it's probably too small for your parakeet. Second, all of that empty space around the bird offers no security if frightened.

Your parakeet's cage is best placed in an area that is going to get *some* traffic — but not too much traffic. *Remember:* You're better off giving your bird too much attention than not enough.

TIP

The cage must be out of drafts and in a consistent temperature zone. If the room has wide temperature swings, you may want to consider a different spot. The bird's room should be dark and quiet for a good part of the night and sunny and bright (with artificial lights, if necessary) for most of the day.

WARNING

There are some places where you should *never* place your parakeet's cage:

>> **A child's bedroom:** Your parakeet won't get a lot of attention in a child's room and will be alone most of the day while your child is at school.

>> **The floor:** A high spot will make your parakeet feel more secure than a low spot, especially if you have other pets.

>> **The bathroom:** This room is prone to wild temperature ranges that aren't good for your parakeet.

>> **The kitchen:** Potential fumes and temperature swings will make your parakeet uncomfortable or ill — and may even kill her. Many products used in the kitchen are not safe for your bird.

>> **Directly in front of a window:** There may be predators outside that can disturb and frighten your bird. Even cars going by can seem dangerous to a little parakeet. Also, older windows can be drafty, especially in winter.

Accessorizing Your Parakeet's Abode

Cage accessories are essential to your parakeet's health and happiness. You may invest in a bunch of accessories in the beginning and then discover that your parakeet needs many more items to make it happy.

Perches, please!

Perches other than those that came with the cage are essential. Your bird spends all of its time on its feet (if your parakeet is lying at the bottom of the cage, feet up, you may want to check to see if he's still breathing!). Because your parakeet uses its feet so much, you want it to be able to stand on perches with as many widths, materials, and textures as possible. (See Figure 4-2.) Think of good perches as orthopedic shoes that can make all the difference between your bird staying healthy and needing a visit to the veterinarian.

Available varieties of perches include

>> **Wooden perches:** Wooden perches come in a variety of shapes, sizes, and types of wood. Regular pine perches are popular and fun for your parakeet to chew. Manzanita perches are harder and last longer; they come in twisty shapes that look more natural than the usual wooden dowels. Cholla wood is also regularly used as perch material and has a natural texture that's good for the feet.

WARNING

You can use perches from your trees outside (see Figure 4-2), but you must be absolutely certain that the type of tree is nontoxic and that it was never sprayed with insecticide, fungicide, or chemical fertilizer.

REMEMBER

Wooden perches need to be cleaned often. Wood is porous and can harbor bad bacteria. Scrub the perches weekly and then soak them in a 10 percent bleach solution once a month (90 parts water, 10 parts bleach). Remember to rinse the perches thoroughly and allow them to dry completely before putting them back into the cage.

>> **Plastic perches:** Plastic perches are popular because they're easy to clean and snap on and off the cage bars easily. These are a fine addition to your array of perches, but they shouldn't be the only kind of perch your bird has. Plastic is probably not as comfortable to stand on as wood or rope.

FIGURE 4-2:
Wooden perches of varying diameters are good for your parakeet's feet.

>> **Rope perches:** Rope perches are made from cotton fibers, sisal, or a hemp-like material. These perches are terrific additions to your parakeet's cage. They come in a variety of diameters and can be twisted into all kinds of shapes to fit into your bird's cage.

WARNING

If you use rope perches, be careful to trim all loose strands that may arise from your parakeet's chewing behavior. These loose stands can wind around a toe, foot, or neck and cause injury. Rope perches should be replaced often, especially if they frequently become damp. If you notice that your parakeet is ingesting the rope, remove it immediately.

>> **Concrete and sand-covered perches:** Concrete and sand-covered perches are available in all sorts of colors and diameters and will often become a bird's favorite perch. This rough perch acts as a nail and beak trimmer. Every parakeet should have at least one of these perches along with the others, ideally two in different diameters. Many birds choose to sleep on the concrete perch at night, so a concrete perch should be the highest perch in the cage.

TIP

Concrete perches are often used as a "napkin" on which your parakeet will wipe its beak after eating a messy meal. This activity is great for the beak but not so great for the perch. Clean the perch often in warm soapy water and be sure to rinse it carefully before placing it back in the cage.

WARNING

Many people are fans of sandpaper sheathes that slip over existing perches. These are actually not great for your parakeet's feet because the sheaths can become soiled easily and can harbor bacteria.

>> **Flat perches:** One flat perch or platform in the cage is good for your parakeet's feet. Often these are made of concrete or sand. Be sure that this perch is high in the cage and not beneath other perches, because a shelf-like perch can become an effective poop catcher. Also, if your parakeets decide to nest on the flat perch and lay eggs and you don't want babies, you may have to remove it.

Cups and bowls

The cage you purchased probably came with a cup for seed and one for water, which is a good start, but you'll need a few more cups to complete your set.

You'll need other types of cups for the various food items you'll be feeding your parakeet. Invest in *mess-free cups* as well — mess-free cups have hoods on them that keep most of the seed, pellets, and other foods inside the cup, not on the floor. These can be real time-savers. However, don't use the hooded cups for water — your bird may crawl inside to take a bath and not be able to get back out. There are hooded, clear plastic bird baths for this purpose.

TIP

Stainless steel is a great material for bird cups because it's durable, easy to clean. Ceramic cups are also a good choice, but if they become cracked or crazed (light, web-like cracking in the glaze), they should be replaced. Both of these types of cups can be found with holders that keep them secure in the cage to avoid seed dumping.

TIP

To save time, keep two sets of dishes. This means that you'll have six dishes — two for seeds/pellets, two for water, and two for fresh foods. Each day, you'll remove the dirty dishes and replace them with the clean dishes, allowing you to disinfect the other dishes for tomorrow.

Cage covers

Some parakeets like their cages to be covered at night, and others may want to be covered only halfway or on three sides. Covering the cage offers a degree of security and protection. Your bird won't be disturbed from sleep by light in the house or a cat slinking around in the middle of the night. The cover protects from drafts as well, and the darkness in the cage may allow you more sleeping time if your bird generally likes to get up with the sun and you don't. Using a cover is like tucking your birds in at night.

Some parakeets will become frightened if their cage is covered all the way. Listen for thrashing and commotion at night. If you sense that your birds are disturbed by the cover, only cover the cage partially so that your parakeet can look out and see what's making that noise at night (probably someone making a midnight snack!).

Swings

Parakeets love swings — there's no doubt about it. Don't scrimp in the swing department. Your parakeet will love a swing with toys and do-dads attached to it — the more the better.

Baths

Bathing is essential for your parakeet — it's good for your parakeet's skin and is a natural behavior, even if it's a bit messy. Don't prevent your bird from bathing, but don't force a bath either.

TIP

Most birds bathe in their water dish, which will require you to clean it more often. Provide your parakeet with a separate bath (larger than the watering dish) that it may prefer.

The standard little bathtub with a mirror in the bottom is particularly popular with parakeets. They can bathe and admire themselves at the same time! You can also buy the kind of hooded bath that hangs outside the cage from one of the doors, a nice option because it keeps the water contained.

You light up my life

If you live in a part of the country that gets cold and dark for a good portion of the year, you'll want to invest in bird lamps, a special wide-spectrum bulb that mimic the sun's rays. There are many made just for birds.

Buy a standard, inexpensive, clamp lamp from the hardware store and clip it a few feet away from your parakeet's cage, shining the bird light directly at the birds. Some of these bulbs offer a bit of heat too, which is great in the wintertime, though you don't want to put the light so close that it heats the birds too much, and make sure that your bird can't get near the bulb, which can be a burning hazard.

TIP

If you can't find bird-specific bulbs, buy bulbs made for reptiles — they're basically the same thing.

Feeling hot hot hot

If you live in a cold climate or you like your air conditioner cranked to freezing, you can purchase a bird heater that attaches directly to the cage bars or walls, allowing your bird to snuggle up to it. There are also heated perches, which many birds really appreciate. You can also use a clamp light and a ceramic reptile bulb that emits heat, but make sure that your bird can't get to it.

Recognizing the Importance of Toys

Toys are vital to the health and well-being of a single parakeet. A pair can get along fairly well without them, but why should they have to? Toys will make up the majority of your parakeet's "job." Wild parakeets work all day at finding food and water and at staying safe. Your parakeet doesn't get nearly this much exercise, though it does require the same amount as its wild cousins. A beloved toy can offer a lonely parakeet a sense of comfort and home.

Typical toys for parakeets

The typical parakeet toy is small, may be plastic or wooden, and often contains a bell. Parakeets love shiny, interactive toys that they can fling around or lavish with affection.

Parakeets are destructive, but they aren't very powerful, which is why there are so many plastic toys on the market geared toward them. These products are fine, but you may want to consider a mixture of wooden, rope, paper, and plastic toys.

WARNING

Mirror toys are popular for the single parakeet. Though this is a fun and interactive toy, your parakeet may become so enamored with its reflection that it forgets about you and its training. Your bird may sit staring into its reflection all day, marveling at what a beautiful and charming mate it has managed to woo. If you notice that Polly is becoming way too affectionate with its mirror, you may want to remove the toy temporarily, until its affections return to you. (See Figure 4-3.)

FIGURE 4-3: Parakeets like mirror toys, just make sure that your bird doesn't become obsessed with it.

Jungle gyms: Not just for gymnasts

A play gym usually consists of a platform affixed with perches, ladders (see Figure 4-4), and toys. This gives your bird ample opportunity to play and get some much-needed activity.

A play gym is also a great training tool because you can place your bird on the steady perch and work with it there, instead of trying to tame or train too close to its cage, where it may seek refuge.

FIGURE 4-4:
Parakeets
love to
climb
around on
ladders
like this
one.

Setting Up the Cage

When you have obtained your cage, you need to set it up properly. Most important is that there are no perches above any food and water dishes. Also, don't crowd the cage. You want to give your bird enough room to exercise without banging into things and possibly becoming injured. Here are a few more steps to make setting up the cage easy:

>> Place a swing directly in the middle of the cage at the top.

>> Place a concrete or sand perch at the highest point in the cage toward the back, leaving enough room for your bird to stand up comfortably. This will likely be the perch where you bird sleeps.

>> Opposite the highest perch, still toward the back, place your flat or platform perch, slightly lower than the sleeping perch.

>> Place your heated perch (if you have one) a few inches away from the sleeping perch at the same level.

>> Place your coop cups for food and water relatively high in the cage. Many cages have spaces for cups at nearly the lowest level in the cage. This only succeeds in soiled food and water.

- ≫ Place perches near the food and water cups to make them easily accessible for your bird.

- ≫ Hang various toys near the base of the perches where they attach to the side of the cage, and a couple of toys near the ends or middle of the perches.

- ≫ Place the seed catcher or bloomer on the cage if you have one.

- ≫ Place a playpen (if you have one) on the top of the cage.

- ≫ Line your cage bottom with paper or litter.

- ≫ Add birds!

Keeping Messes at Bay

Even if you have only one parakeet, it may seem that the mess in your home has doubled. You can't keep your parakeet from making messes, but you can contain the mess.

The most surefire way of keeping your floor clean is to not allow the seed to fall there in the first place. Cage bloomers and seed guards, available at your local pet shop, can be a huge help. Both products fit snugly around the cage bottom and create a barrier so that most of the seed stays in the cage tray.

TIP

If your birds are determined to make a mess regardless of the bloomer, you can purchase a few yards of clear plastic, the kind someone may use for a tablecloth. It's nontoxic and easy to handle. Cover three of the four sides of your cage with this material and it may stop the mess by 90 percent. Leave the top and the front of the cage uncovered, but place a flap of the plastic in front, where the food and water dishes are. It works very well. A more expensive mess-busting idea is to purchase an acrylic cage, which is a more attractive possibility.

TIP

By far, the handiest item in your cleaning kit is the handheld vacuum. This little machine is your remedy to utter disarray. An automatic robot vacuum is also handy.

Many household cleansers are deadly to your bird, so don't use them in or around your bird's cage. Instead, use natural disinfectants such as vinegar for cleaning the cage and baking soda for scrubbing. If you have a real mess, you can use a 10 percent bleach solution for soaking (1 cup bleach per 10 cups water), but always make sure to rinse very carefully before returning anything soaked in bleach to your bird.

TIP

You can buy special bird-safe cleaners at the pet shop or online, which work rather well and often smell pretty good. Nothing makes up for good old elbow grease and safe household cleansers like vinegar or baking soda — don't mix vinegar and baking soda, though, or you'll get an interesting chemical reaction that may force you to do more cleaning!

REMEMBER

Clean the paper in the bottom of the cage every day if you can or at least every other day, about 3 to 4 times a week. Scrape off any dried droppings once a week and soak the entire cage in soapy water or a 10 percent bleach solution about every ten days. Removing the dried feces from the cage will prevent it from aerosolizing (becoming powdery and airborne), which can then be inhaled by both your birds and yourself and your family.

Speaking of air . . . parakeets, like most birds, generate dander from their feathers and create feather dust, which can float on the air and be inhaled. To prevent this, place a HEPA filter near the cage to keep your air clean. Make sure not to turn on an ion or ozone feature if it has one, as ozone can be deadly to birds when inhaled.

Parakeet-Proofing Your Home

If you're going to allow your parakeet time out of the cage, even if you think that you're going to supervise it all the time, you have to parakeet-proof your home. Even if you have a pair that isn't going to leave the cage, the average home has items that can be harmful, even deadly, to a parakeet, even one inside a cage where it seems safe. In the following sections, I cover tips to keep your home safe for your new companion.

Make sure all windows are screened

Parakeets are excellent flyers, and even a partially clipped parakeet will be able to soar away. Many people lose their parakeets through an open window or door, especially if more than one person lives in the household. One person may open a window and another person may let the bird out of the cage, neither aware of what the other has done.

Either keep your parakeet's wings clipped or build a flight cage or aviary where your birds can fly safely without the danger of flying away. Be sure that your aviary is predator-safe and has shelter from the elements.

Keep your windows and mirrors a little dirty

Your parakeet will think that a window or mirror is actually more space, and the bird may soar right into it. Keeping your windows and your mirrors dirty is a great way to help avoid this kind of heartbreaking accident.

If you like your windows spotless, place gel stickers on your windows and mirrors to help your bird distinguish between a hard surface and more flying space.

Get rid of (or at least turn off) the ceiling fan

Ceiling fans are an absolute no-no when it comes to your parakeet. (See Figure 4-5.) Your parakeet may fly up there while it's on and get injured, or worse. One whoosh of a whirling blade and he's history. Keep ceiling fans off when your parakeet is out of the cage, or better yet, disable them or remove the fan blades.

FIGURE 4-5:
Be very careful if you have flighted parakeets and ceiling fans.

Keep your house free of artificial scents

Parakeets have an extremely delicate respiratory system. Scents that may not bother you — like those from a scented candle or an air freshener — can kill a parakeet. Potpourri in a bowl might look like a fun snack, as will scented wax beads. Keep all of these items away from your parakeet's area.

Avoid all products with nonstick coatings

When it's heated, some nonstick coatings, like PTFE, used on many types of cookware and other products emits a fume that has been proven to kill birds, so be sure never to use such products as long as you're a bird owner.

WARNING

Even if your parakeet is in another part of the house from where you're cooking, the fumes still travel — these fumes have been known to kill birds through walls in apartment buildings.

TIP

Products that use nonstick coating (and that should be avoided at all costs) include the following:

- Air fryers
- Bread machines
- Broiler pans
- Coffeemakers
- Cooking utensils (with nonstick coating, silicone is ok)
- Crock pots
- Curling irons
- Deep fryers
- Drip pans for burners
- Electric skillets
- Griddles
- Hairdryers with nonstick coils
- Heat lamps
- Instapots (replace the interior pot with a stainless steel pot to make it safer)
- Ironing-board covers
- Irons
- Lollipop molds
- Ovens with nonstick coating (which burns off after the first use or when being self-cleaned; never self-clean your oven with your bird in the house)
- Pizza pans
- Popcorn poppers
- Portable heaters
- Roasters
- Rolling pins (the nonstick variety)
- Stockpots
- Stovetop burners
- Waffle makers
- Woks

I know this list is long, and it may seem that you have to change your whole life for your parakeet. Some people do use some of these items successfully if their homes are very well ventilated and the nonstick item is being used far away from the parakeet. You can also keep a safe cage in your yard or on your balcony for when you cook using non-stick items. In any case, the most crucial of these is the cookware — most bird keepers don't use it.

Make sure your parakeet doesn't have access to standing water

Fish tanks, toilet bowls, indoor and table-top fountains, and even your dog's water dish all pose a drowning threat to a parakeet.

Parakeets can even drown in a glass of water while trying to take a drink. Cover all standing water.

Put your bird away while cooking. Birds have been known to get inquisitive about a pot of boiling water, oil, or sauce, to deadly consequences.

Remove all toxic houseplants from your parakeet's reach

Some houseplants are perfectly safe for nibbling and others are extremely deadly. If you don't know whether a plant is toxic, do an online search for plants that are safe or unsafe for birds, or simply don't let your bird near plants at all.

Your parakeet may like to chew on tree cuttings from the outdoors, but be absolutely sure that the branches you offer are non-toxic and have not been sprayed with *any* kind of pesticides, fungicides, or fertilizers — these chemicals can be instantly deadly to your parakeet.

Other Pets and Your Parakeet

Other pets pose a grave danger to your parakeet. Dogs and cats are *predators* and parakeets are *prey*. This means that even your sweet, loving Fido or Fluffy may want to kill and eat your parakeet. They can't help it; preying on small, fast-moving animals is their natural instinct. Your parakeet's entire being is as a small, fast-moving object.

WARNING

Cats have a type of bacteria on their claws and teeth called *Pasteurella* that is deadly to birds. If your cat even nicks your parakeet with one little claw, your bird is in trouble. Never, ever, *ever* allow your cat access to your parakeet. You'll see cute videos online of small birds hanging around with cats, so what's the big deal, right? For every cute video, I guarantee that there are hundreds (maybe thousands) of horror stories about the comingling of cats and companion birds.

Some dogs, like terriers, are bred to chase small, fast-moving objects. Other dogs, like spaniels, poodles, and retrievers, are actually bred to hunt and retrieve birds. Other breeds are content to think of your parakeet not as a meal, but as toy, and this is not a good scenario either. As they say . . . I've seen some things. Don't trust your bird around your dog.

WARNING

If you have a big dog, be sure that your parakeet can't get to the water dish — these little birds have been known to drown in deep dog bowls.

Other birds

People often keep parakeets in aviaries with other birds. I've seen parakeets living peacefully with cockatiels, canaries, and finches. *Remember:* You need a lot of space in order for all these birds to get along.

Some birds can be quite vicious and dangerous to your parakeet. Lovebirds, for example, will not tolerate any other bird species in their vicinity. A larger parrot may also take offense at your parakeet's presence and easily kill your little bird.

REMEMBER

Before you bring another bird home to your existing birds, you must set up a place where you can *quarantine* (isolate) the new bird. This place should be well away from your other birds, and you should care for the new bird last and wash yourself and your clothes after each interaction. Quarantine traditionally lasts 40 days, though some people quarantine for only 30 days as long as there are no signs of illness.

2

Caring for Your Parakeet

IN THIS CHAPTER

» Feeding your parakeet properly

» Learning about supplements

» Cooking for your parakeet

Chapter **5**

Polly Want a Cracker? Feeding Your Parakeet Properly

P arakeets are prone to nutritional disorders, many of which can be deadly. They are notorious for gorging on seed to the exclusion of just about everything else if you let them. Obesity is a huge (pardon the pun) health issue for parakeets, so it's important to ensure that your bird gets the proper nutrition.

Water, Water Everywhere . . .

In the wild, parakeets base their daily activities on finding water, flying for many miles each day to drink. The wild parakeet's breeding season revolves around rain, and the number of chicks successfully hatched is dependent on how much water is available to the parents.

WARNING

Try not to use water straight from the tap as your bird's drinking water. Tap water contains chlorine, metals, and other toxins, which are bad for your parakeet. Bottled drinking water or filtered water is a much better option unless you are absolutely sure that the water from your tap is safe.

TIP

To remove chlorine from tap water, simply fill up a container with water (a glass or plastic gallon bottle is a good option) and allow it to stand on your kitchen counter for 24 hours minimum and up to five days if you want all the chlorine to evaporate. If you are leaving the bottle for more than 24 hours, use a piece of cheesecloth and a rubber band to cover the top so that contaminants and thirsty insects don't fall in.

WARNING

Do not let your parakeet's water become filthy. Change your bird's water no less than once a day, and twice a day if you can. Dirty water can harbor bacteria that are potentially harmful for your bird. Your parakeet's water dishes should be clean enough for *you* to drink out of them.

TIP

An easy way to ensure that your bird's water remains fresh is to have two sets of water dishes — one for the morning water change and one for the evening water change. Soak water dishes in a 10 percent bleach solution (one part bleach to nine parts water) once a week to sterilize them. Rinse the water dishes thoroughly before returning them to your parakeet's cage.

WARNING

If you have a tube-style waterer, or a product called a "two-week waterer," you still must change the water daily. If you don't, your parakeet could get sick. Just because the package says "two-week waterer" doesn't mean that you don't have to change the water for two weeks! Water bottles can also get clogged and contaminated, use a bottle brush to scrub them out whenever they are changed. I recommend sticking with water bowls and just cleaning them more often.

FeedingYour Parakeet

WARNING

Companion parakeets do well on a seed-*based* diet because they are primarily ground-foraging seed eaters in the wild (along with berries, fruit, and flower buds), but they can't live on seeds alone. (See Figure 5-1.) Seed is full of carbs and fat, and only a lifestyle high in exercise (like the kind of lifestyle wild parakeets have) can burn off all those calories. An all-seed diet will cause your parakeet to develop serious health issues and will shorten its already short life by *years.*

In the following sections, I let you know what kinds of foods your parakeet needs and wants, what foods you should *never* feed your parakeet, and how to supplement your parakeet's diet.

FIGURE 5-1:
Parakeets are ground feeders, meaning that they naturally fly to the ground to forage.

What to feed your parakeet

Each species of bird has its own dietary requirements, and the parakeet is no exception. In the following sections, I cover the many kinds of foods you can and should feed your parakeet.

TIP

No matter what kind of food you offer your parakeet, always give as much as the bird will eat. You don't have to ration your bird's feed the way you might have to ration a dog or cat. The only time you may want to ration is with seeds, and in this case you will be replacing the seeds with other foods, so your parakeet should never go hungry. Parakeets have a very fast metabolism, and even one day without food can cause problems — longer than that can cause death.

Seeds

TIP

Because parakeets are ground foraging seed eaters in the wild, your pet parakeet will relish seed. I recommend that you *do* offer seed in small amounts, but not as the bird's entire diet. Your veterinarian may suggest that you don't feed seed at all, and that choice is up to you. If you convert your bird to another type of base diet — pellets, for example — then there is no reason to offer seeds beyond the fact that your bird likes them.

Many veterinarians suggest that people take their birds off of seeds because they feel that owners may not be responsible enough to provide a diverse and healthful diet for their birds. Parakeets are seed eaters in the wild, however, so seeds are a natural part of their diet, but if you are also conscientious about offering fresh foods, seeds can be a good base diet.

TIP

Some of the seed mixes in the pet shop are brightly colored and claim to be "fortified" with vitamins. The fact is that the vitamins are in the coloring that the manufacturer coats on the *outside* of the seed, while the inside of the seed, the only part that your parakeet actually eats, remains the same. Save your money and buy the regular seed packaged for parakeets and spend the savings on healthy fruits and vegetables for your bird instead.

WARNING

Parakeets open seeds to eat the nutritious center of the seed, leaving behind the husk, which is inedible. Seed husks will likely stay inside the seed dish, making the dish look full all the time, even though all of the edible parts of the seeds have been eaten. Don't be fooled into thinking that a full dish means that your parakeet doesn't need more food. I actually saw a parakeet guardian nearly starve their bird to death by thinking that the seed dish was full and not adding fresh seed. Blow off the chaff and top up the seed dish every day, toss it all once a week, wash the dish, and start filling it again.

Seeds that have been sprouted are much higher in nutrition than dry seeds and make a nutritious treat. You can find already sprouted seeds at the supermarket (broccoli, mung bean, and wheat grass, for example) or you can sprout your own.

Pellets

Pellets emerged on the bird scene a number of years ago and have quickly become a trend in feeding birds. Pellets are a combination of ingredients that the manufacturer shapes into bits that resemble seeds and other shapes that birds find interesting.

As with seeds, pellets are not *bad,* but they are not the only food you should feed your parakeet. Variety is essential. Pellets are an okay base diet, but feeding them does not mean that you should exclude other foods, such as fruits and vegetables, table foods, and some seeds.

Check the label on the pellets, and try to buy only all-natural, preservative-free, dye-free, organic pellets. Make sure that the pellets are formulated specifically for parakeets and are the appropriate size for parakeets.

Fruits and vegetables

Vegetables and fruits are a great way to get important vitamins and minerals into your parakeet, and they make a fun addition to the diet as well. Try to feed your parakeet at least five types fresh vegetables or fruits a day. (See Figure 5-2.) Eventually, you'll get to know what your parakeet's favorites are and you can keep them on hand.

How you serve fruits and veggies depends on the type of fruit or veggie. For example, your parakeet may like broccoli florets, apple wedges, shredded cabbage, whole or shredded greens (leaves), peas out of the pod, chopped green beans, and carrots (whole, chopped, shredded, or cooked). Experiment with how you serve fruits and veggies. If your parakeet doesn't eat it one way, your bird may be tempted to try the food item another way. Also, when serving fruit, make sure to remove any seeds or pits, as these can be toxic.

Here's a list of vegetables that are good for your parakeet:

- ➤ beans (cooked)
- ➤ broccoli
- ➤ cabbage
- ➤ carrots
- ➤ cauliflower
- ➤ cucumbers
- ➤ endive
- ➤ green beans
- ➤ greens (all varieties)
- ➤ hot peppers
- ➤ kale
- ➤ peas
- ➤ potato (cooked)
- ➤ pumpkin
- ➤ soybeans
- ➤ spinach
- ➤ squash
- ➤ watercress
- ➤ yams
- ➤ zucchini

Here's a list of fruits that are good for your parakeet:

- ➤ apples
- ➤ bananas
- ➤ berries (all varieties)
- ➤ cantaloupes
- ➤ figs
- ➤ grapes (with skin)
- ➤ honeydew
- ➤ kiwis
- ➤ mangoes
- ➤ oranges
- ➤ peaches
- ➤ pears
- ➤ pineapples
- ➤ plums
- ➤ tangerines

Deep green or orange produce have the most nutrients, especially vitamin A, which your parakeet needs to be healthy. Vitamin A-deficient birds are prone to respiratory problems and skin and liver problems.

REMEMBER

Wash all fruit and vegetables thoroughly before serving. Your parakeet can be affected by even the tiniest traces of pesticides, fungicides, and chemical fertilizers. If you can, offer organic produce so you have one less thing to worry about. A good wash for produce is a vinegar solution. Pour one cup of white vinegar into a spray bottle with three cups of water and a tablespoon of lemon juice. Spray liberally over your fruits and veggies and rinse.

WARNING

Fruits and vegetables sour quickly in warm weather, so remove them a few hours after you offer them if you live in a warm climate and your birds are outdoors. You can leave these foods in the cage longer in cooler weather or in air conditioning, but if you put them out in the morning in any climate, make sure to remove them in the evening.

FIGURE 5-2: Parakeets should be given greens and other fruits and veggies every day.

Snacks

TIP

There are a lot of commercially made bird snacks available, many of them seed-based. Your parakeet will relish a snack like this, but realize that your bird may prefer it to healthier foods (just as you may prefer chocolate to cauliflower). Only offer a seed-based treat to your parakeet after it has eaten its fresh foods for the day or during training sessions.

Millet spray is another treat that your parakeet will *love*. The millet spray looks like a little tree branch with hundreds of seeds attached to it (see Figure 5-3). Again, don't let your bird gorge on it. Offer millet spray once or twice a week, or a small part of a spray as a treat just before bed.

FIGURE 5-3:
Parakeets
love millet
spray as a
treat.

Table foods

TIP

Healthy table foods are a wonderful addition to your parakeet's diet. With a few exceptions, your bird can eat anything that you eat. Unlike dogs and cats, which can become ill from table foods, your parakeet may actually become healthier if you share your meals. And don't worry about spices — birds can eat the hottest of peppers because they have far fewer taste buds than we do.

TIP

Eggs are also a great addition to your bird's diet, in any style. One great way to serve eggs is to boil them for about 30 minutes, cool them, and then crush them, shell and all (the shell contains much-needed calcium). *Remember:* Make sure to boil the eggs well because those eggs came from a chicken that could potentially pass on a disease to your parakeet.

Your parakeet may enjoy your breakfast cereal, especially Cheerios, because it can hold the little Os in its beak and tote them around the cage. In the cold months, offer hot cereal, such as oatmeal, prepared and then cooled to just above room temperature.

"Birds eating birds" sounds like a sleazy talk-show topic, but in this case I'm referring to feeding your parakeet chicken and turkey meat. Believe it or not, a bit of these foods on occasion is healthy, adding some protein to your parakeet's diet.

Limited amounts of whole-wheat and nutty-grain bread is a great snack every other day for non-breeding birds. It's especially good if you are breeding your parakeets because it's soft and easy to feed to the babies. Whole-wheat crackers are good, too, but be sure that they're not salty — salt-free crackers are best. Even low-sodium crackers may contain too much salt for your parakeets.

Cooked foods

Several manufacturers have come out with a cooked food product for birds that you prepare once or twice a week and serve warm. Parakeets, as well as other birds, absolutely love this kind of food.

TIP

You'd do well to make these cooked diets the bird's base diet and offer fewer seeds and pellets. See later in this chapter for some cooked diet recipes.

What not to feed your parakeet

Though *you* may eat a Twinkie or two or a whole bag of chips or carton of ice cream while watching television, that doesn't mean your bird can share in these treats. *Never* indulge your bird with junk food of any kind. Salty, fatty, and sugary foods are terrible for your parakeet — they can even be deadly.

WARNING

Birds can actually die from foods that we humans eat regularly. Here is a list of the *nevers* and why you shouldn't feed them:

>> **Alcohol:** Put your bird on the wagon and don't ever share your margarita with him! Alcohol is toxic to birds and can cause death.

>> **Avocado:** This tasty plant harbors an ingredient near the near the pit that is toxic to birds. Don't take the chance.

>> **Caffeine:** Never give your bird sips of soda, tea, or coffee. Caffeine is toxic to birds. Herbal tea, such as chamomile, can be a healthy, warm beverage alternative for your parakeet.

>> **Chocolate:** Birds metabolize chocolate differently from humans, and the result is toxic.

>> **Onions and garlic (raw):** Well-cooked onions and garlic in something you're eating and want to share will probably be

fine, but never feed your parakeet raw onions or garlic. (If you want to be safe, just avoid onions and garlic altogether.)

>> **Pits and fruit seeds:** Remove all seeds and pits from fruits before you serve them to your parakeet. Some of these seeds are toxic.

>> **Rhubarb:** This delicious vegetable can be toxic to your bird.

Nutritional supplements: When food isn't enough

Like humans, parakeets can often benefit from dietary supplements. In the following sections, I cover some ways in which you may want to supplement your parakeet's diet.

Do not supplement before you speak to your avian veterinarian.

>> **Vitamin A:** Parrot-type birds, such as your parakeet, need more vitamin A in their diet than humans do. Talk to your veterinarian about your parakeet's diet and the possibility of adding an emulsified vitamin A supplement to the water. Your avian veterinarian may opt for a better diet for your parakeet rather than a supplement.

Vitamin A is toxic at high levels. Before you consider offering a supplement, try to get your parakeet to eat fruits and vegetables that are rich in vitamin A, such as carrots and their tops, dandelion greens, sweet potatoes, kale, spinach, butternut squash, mangoes, red peppers, and turnip greens.

Liquid or powdered vitamins tend to turn a parakeet's water into a bacteria soup. If you do decide to add vitamins to your parakeet's water, be sure that you change the water at least twice a day. Or, add a powdered multi-vitamin/mineral supplement to the fresh offering or the soft food.

Many bird keepers add one or two drops of apple cider vinegar to their bird's water daily. The vinegar is said to ward off bacteria and is even healthful for your bird. Be careful not to add too much, or the water will be too stinky to drink. Purchase organic apple cider vinegar if you can.

A drop or two of grapefruit seed extract in the water will help keep bacteria from growing too rapidly in the water and it's healthy for your bird. Just don't use too much in relation to the amount of water because it has a bitter taste.

>> **Powdered additives:** Because seeds lack many nutrients, you can purchase a powdered additive that you sprinkle onto your bird's food. The problem with putting this powder on seeds is that the powder often sifts through the seed and is not ingested by your bird, so it's best placed on cooked diets or fruits and veggies. When used in conjunction with an oil-based supplement (see the preceding section), the powder will stick, making the seed a nutrient-rich food.

>> **Cuttlebones and mineral blocks:** Cuttlebone is a good source of natural calcium. It actually comes from inside of a cuttlefish, a type of squid. Hang the cuttlebone on the side of the cage near a perch, and watch your parakeet pick at it and play with it.

TIP

Some people are concerned with the source of the cuttlebone, fearing that the squid may have been harvested in polluted waters. If you want, you can opt instead for a mineral block, which is a good source of calcium (many contain other minerals as well). You can also use a mineral block in conjunction with a cuttlebone. A mineral block may also help keep the beak trim.

TECHNICAL STUFF

KISS MY GRITS!

A common myth is that all birds need grit in their diet. Parakeets absolutely do *not* need it. Because parakeets *hull* their seeds (remove the outer shell from the seed and eat only the seed itself), the bird has no need for any kind of sand in the *gizzard* (the bird's "second stomach" that grinds the food). In fact, the presence of grit in the cage may incite the bird to gorge on it, stuffing up its digestive system with stones that won't come out, which can lead to health problems and death. The bottom line: Do not offer grit to your parakeet.

Making Some Fun and Nutritious Recipes for Your Parakeet

It's not easy to get birds to eat healthy. Cooking for your bird can help it get the nutrients it needs. Here are some fun, flexible recipes to get you started.

Budgie mash

A mash of beans and grains is very healthy for your parakeet. You can offer a commercially prepared grain mix (find in pet stores or online), but if you want to get creative, you can make up a batch of this once a month and freeze 30 portions of it in ice trays, then heat up one mash cube a day for consumption.

Using the directions on the boxes, make a serving each of quinoa, amaranth, brown rice, whole oats, and whole-wheat couscous (use some or all, it's a very flexible recipe). Cook separately, then blend them all together once they're done. Add cooked whole wheat pasta as well if you like.

Soak and cook a few types of small beans, such as lentils and black-eyed peas. Or, if you're in a hurry, open a few cans of beans, rinse them, and then add them to the grain mixture. You can also sprout the beans before you add them.

Finally, add some shredded carrots, yams, chopped jalapeno peppers, peas, broccoli, kale, frozen soybeans, frozen peas, and anything else you have in the house that's healthy and safe to feed your parakeet. Toss in some slivered or chopped almonds, chopped walnuts, organic pellets, and anything else that seems to belong in the mix. Add a sprinkle of cinnamon, calcium powder, and any other dry supplements you have on hand. Heat on a plate in the microwave to slightly above room temperature and offer one serving a day. Don't serve too hot!

This recipe can actually be used as your parakeet's base diet, and you can offer pellets and seeds as a treat.

Parakeet pancakes and waffles

Find a whole-wheat or buckwheat pancake or waffle mix. Make the batter as directed on the box, and then add chopped dried fruit, veggies like chopped broccoli, pre-boiled or roasted crushed eggshells, pellets, millet, and anything healthful you have in the house (remember that wet ingredients may make the pancake mix too moist). Cook well and cool before offering. Freeze and offer a part of thawed pancake or waffle a day along with other foods. Because your bird is small, see if you can make tiny pancakes. Remember, most waffle irons have non-stick coating, so make sure that your bird isn't near the kitchen or is in a well-ventilated area before you break out the waffle maker.

Budgie muffins

Corn-muffin mix with lots of goodies added equals an easy, nutritious snack. Purchase a box of corn-muffin mix and follow the directions for the batter. If you can find a mix from a health food store or a healthier version online, use it instead of the supermarket brand, or you can make corn muffins from scratch.

WARNING

If your parakeet has candida (yeast), skip this recipe until it gets over the infection, or make sure that the mix you use doesn't include sugar.

TIP

Using the directions on the box, prepare the batter, and if it calls for an egg, smash the shell in there with the rest of it, and then add several different healthy items: fruits, veggies, dried fruit, pellets, bits of cuttlebone, whatever you think your bird will love. Then bake according to the directions on the box, but double the baking time, or check a few times to make sure it's done. The added water in the fruits and veggies will add time to baking. Once cooled, cut into squares and freeze. Each day, thaw a chunk and offer it to your parakeet along with its regular food. These muffins are fun because you can vary the recipe each time you make it.

Parakeet scramble

Chicken eggs are a good source of protein, vitamins, and minerals for your parakeet. Make scrambled eggs just as you would for yourself, but scramble the shell with them (for calcium), and add pellets, veggies, and whatever else you think your bird will like. Cook eggs very well until dry. You can make a batch and freeze in small portions for later use.

WARNING

Whenever you use chicken eggs, ensure that they're cooked extremely well. Chicken eggs can carry diseases that can pass to your parakeet. Scrambled eggs should be very dry, and boiled eggs should be cooked for 20 minutes or more to remove any Salmonella bacteria.

Parakeet juice and smoothies

If you have a juicer, fresh-pressed juice is full of a lot of vitamins and minerals that are essential for your parakeet's good health. Press carrots, beets, apples, melon, kale, chard, mint, spinach, broccoli, Brussels sprouts, and any other fruits and veggies your bird likes. You can make the recipes as simple or complex as you like. Because juice spoils easily, don't place the juice in the bird's cage, but rather offer it to the bird during playtime.

TIP

If you don't have a juicer, use a blender. Rather than juice fruits and veggies, blend them into a smoothie, which has some benefits over juicing:

>> Your parakeet gets the benefit of the fiber that's lost with juicing.

>> You can also add powders and harder foods, like coconut or nuts, and vegan yogurt. Flax seeds, chia seeds, powdered vitamin C, calcium, powdered or liquid minerals, and anything else you're having a tough time getting your bird to eat are also good additions.

To make the smoothie even more nutritious, juice first and use that liquid as a base for the smoothie.

Chapter **6**

Pretty Bird! Grooming Your Parakeet

You may not have taken grooming into consideration when you bought your parakeet. But just like a dog or a long-haired cat, a parakeet needs some extra, above-and-beyond care to live a long and happy life. In fact, proper and regular grooming is an integral part of good parakeet care.

Thinking about Feathers

A healthy parakeet will keep itself clean. You will notice your bird running its beak through its feathers. This is called preening and is a normal behavior. Your parakeet is making sure that its feathers are clean and tidy. (See Figure 6-1.) A bird with dirty feathers can't fly well, resist moisture, or regulate its temperature, all things that feathers offer a bird.

Feathers are made of *keratin*, the same material that makes up their beaks (as well as our fingernails and other animals' horns) and are over 90 percent protein. Parakeets have several types of feathers. Here are a few you should know:

>> **Contour feathers** cover your parakeet's body and include the flight feathers and the tail feathers.

>> **Flight feathers** are responsible for flight. The wing composed of 20 flight feathers: ten primary flight feathers (the long feathers at the end of the wing) and ten secondary flight feathers (closer to the body). Also called *remiges*.

>> **Tail feathers** are called *retrices*.

>> **Semiplume** feathers occur underneath the contour feathers and help with insulation.

>> **Filoplumes** are hairlike feathers that have a long shaft with a few *barbs* at the end (see next section for a definition of *barb*). They are "sensory" feathers used to help the bird feel the positions of its other feathers while adjusting air pressure during flight.

>> **Bristles** are the stiff, tiny feathers around your parakeet's beak, nares (nostrils), and eyes.

>> **Down** is the undercoat of fluffy feathers beneath the contour feathers are called the down feathers. These help a great deal with insulation.

The feather itself is made up of five basic components:

>> **The quill** is the hollow lower end of the feather under the skin follicle; also called the *calamus*.

>> **The shaft** continues above the skin appearing as the feather's dividing central stem; is also called the *rachis*.

>> **Barbs** are the thin strands emanating from the shaft.

>> **Barbules** are tiny structures emanating from the barbs. Down feathers do not have barbules and therefore aren't neatly "zipped" like the contour feathers.

>> **Barbicels** are tiny hooks attached to the barbules that keep the barbs together to form the feather. There are about 30 million barbicels on one feather.

FIGURE 6-1:
A healthy
parakeet's
feathers
are clean
and sleek,
like with
this female
and male
pair.

Grooming Your Parakeet

A healthy parakeet will preen itself to keep its feathers clean and sleek. You don't need to do much to the feathers aside from offering clean water for a bath and maybe trimming the flight feathers.

Bathing your bird

Parakeets love to bathe, and watching them happily splashing away in a bird bath is a treat. A shallow dish of tepid water should get your parakeet in the mood to bathe. (See Figure 6-2.) Many parakeet owners use misters or spray bottles to bathe their birds, whereas others find that running the faucet on low in the kitchen sink and holding the bird near the water helps to prompt bathing (and it's very cute!).

TIP

Encourage bathing in the daylight hours so that your bird doesn't go to sleep wet.

You may not think that a bird bathing in winter is a good idea, but it's actually fine. Your home may be very dry in winter and the bird may need to moisten its skin. Birds generally know what's best when it comes to bathing, so trust your parakeet's instincts.

TIP

You don't need to blow-dry or towel-dry your parakeet (and blow-drying can be deadly if your blow-dryer has nonstick coating on its coils). Provide a warm lamp for the bird to sidle up to if he's cold or offer a heated perch or bird heater. *Remember:* If you provide a lamp, make sure it's not too close! The bird should be able to move at least 18 inches away from it. Healthy birds generally dry pretty quickly anyway, in a half hour or so in most weather.

WARNING

You may find some bathing products at the pet store or online that claim to be good for a bird's skin and feathers. These products may actual irritate your parakeet's eyes if you spray the product in them. Read product labels and use your best judgment, or save your money and use good old-fashioned water.

Another way to encourage your parakeet to bathe is to offer a shallow dish of wet greens, such as water cress, arugula, or baby spinach, at the bottom of the cage. Parakeets will often jump into the greens to bathe, and may also enjoy nibbling on and playing with them.

FIGURE 6-2: Offering your parakeet a separate bath encourages it to bathe there rather than in the water dish.

Wing clipping

Wing clipping is when someone cuts off the ends of the first seven of the ten primary (or flight) feathers of the wing so that the bird won't be able to fly high, but instead will gently flutter to the ground. This practice is common among parakeet owners and is a painless procedure for the bird, equivalent to a human getting a haircut, except that you don't move around with the use of your hair.

REMEMBER

Like human hair, flight feathers grow back. You can expect the flight feathers to be back in about five to six months, or after a *molt*, or loss and re-growth of feathers (see the nearby sidebar, "Molting parakeets," for more information). The feathers that you cut won't regrow, they have to fall out first. If you want to keep your parakeet's wings clipped, make sure to check the flight feathers every month to make sure none have grown out. (See Figure 6-3.)

FIGURE 6-3:
This parakeet is molting. You can see the new pin feathers peeking through the existing feathers on this bird's head and face.

Ah, that is the question! Wing clipping is a much-heated discussion among bird enthusiasts. Some are in favor of clipping and some are against it. Wherever you fall in the argument, you'll have to make a decision about wing clipping. A clipped bird *is* easier to tame, but that doesn't mean that your bird must be clipped for its entire life. Clipping is a personal decision and you'll have to live with the consequences if something happens to your bird, whether it's is clipped or not.

WHAT ABOUT THE BEAK?

Most veterinarians recommend that bird owners do *not* trim the beak. You can harm your bird drastically by trimming the beak. If your parakeet's beak seems overgrown, the bird may have a serious health disorder that needs to be addressed by a veterinarian. The doctor can help your bird with the health problem and trim the beak at the same time. Malnutrition, mites, and an injury can all contribute to beak over-growth.

A healthy bird does things with its beak that will naturally wear it down, such as eating hard foods, playing with toys, wiping its beak on perches, and chewing on wood. You can bet that there's a problem if your parakeet's beak needs trimming.

Birds get more exercise and are happier when they can fly. I'd rather take every precaution so that my birds don't get hurt and keep them fully flighted, but I'm just one voice among many. Ultimately, you need to do what's right for you and your bird. Though a clipped bird can be easier to handle and won't fly away, an unclipped bird can get into trouble in the average home and may find its way out an open window and disappear.

Clipping should allow your parakeet to flutter gently to the floor. If you cut too much, there is the potential for injury. Too little, and the bird could still take off into the wild blue yonder.

TIP

Watch someone experienced in clipping, like an avian veterinarian, a breeder, or a bird-shop owner, clip your bird the first time. You can also find instructional videos online, but I recommend you watch someone clip in person at least once. You won't ever have to clip your bird yourself if you can find someone in your area who will charge you a few dollars for clipping.

MOLTING PARAKEETS

Molting is when a bird loses some of the old feathers on its body and grows new feathers. When your parakeet is molting, you'll notice more feathers than usual on the floor of the cage, but you shouldn't be able to notice any bald patches or feather loss on the bird himself. If you do, take your bird to an avian veterinarian right away.

Molting birds are going through a rough, cranky time. Their skin may itch and the new feathers breaking out of their skin may even be painful. This is not the time to try a new training method or make any changes to your bird's housing.

A companion bird may molt once or twice a year, depending on the weather and lighting where you live. Molting is seasonal, but for birds living inside, it can occur any time. Molting can last a few weeks to a few months.

A molting bird will appreciate a daily bath or a spraying. The bath helps to soften the sheaths over the *pin feathers* (the newly grown feathers, also referred to as *blood feathers* because they have a blood supply) and helps the new feather emerge.

Molting birds need extra nutritional support. Many bird keepers offer their molting birds a product called egg food, which you can buy from your local pet store or online. This product looks like crumbly yellow breadcrumbs and contains a lot of vitamins and minerals that a molting bird needs. A quick online search will bring up recipes for egg food that you can make at home. Egg food is also good for breeding pairs and their babies.

If you are new to clipping a bird's flight feathers, then it's a job for two people, one to hold the parakeet gently in a small hand towel and one to clip the wings. Note that it's crucial not to hold the bird too tightly. Birds breathe differently than we do and any pressure around the body can prevent breathing. You can safely hold the bird cradled with its back against the inside of your palm, folding three fingers across the lower body without restricting the chest, and firmly hold its head between your forefinger and your thumb. Be gentle. Extend one wing at a time to begin. Search online for videos on how to properly hold a parakeet or budgie during wing clipping.

With the wing spread, you'll see the primary flight feathers at the end of the wing, with the shorter feathers, the *coverts*, covering the upper part of the flight feathers — never cut these shorter feathers (see Figure 6-4)! Cut the flight feathers parallel to the coverts, about 2 millimeters away from them. Never, *ever* cut into a feather inside a sheath. This is a "living" feather, a blood feather, and will bleed (see the nearby sidebar, "Beware blood feathers"). The sheath looks like thin, white plastic covering the rolled-up feather and coming to a point, like a pin (hence, the name *pin feather*).

Use a small, sharp cuticle scissor for wing clipping, not an office or kitchen scissor, which may be dull and can mangle the feathers instead of giving a clean cut. If the cut is ragged, it can irritate the bird and may cause feather plucking or self-mutilation.

TIP

Only trim feathers in a clean, well-lighted place where you can see what you're doing. If you can't see well, you could potentially harm your little bird with those sharp scissors. Always keep a *bird-safe* styptic powder (which you can get at a local pet shop or online) on hand in case you accidentally clip a blood feather. You can also use baking flour or corn starch, which may be easier on the skin. Styptic powder for human use can burn the skin.

Trim the feathers on both wings evenly. Don't trim only one wing. If the wings are uneven, the parakeet can't control its descent, and could injure itself trying to land. Some people will advise to leave the first two primary flight feathers intact, but this isn't a recommended practice because your parakeet could break these feathers easily, as they are no longer protected by the surrounding feathers.

Toenail clipping

Your parakeet may develop sharp little toenails, which will make your relationship with the bird slightly unpleasant if this is a bird you handle often. You don't want to be scratched painfully when you're playing with your bird. Even though your parakeet may have a concrete perch, which is great for keeping the nails trimmed, you may have to manually trim the nails as well.

Wing clipping

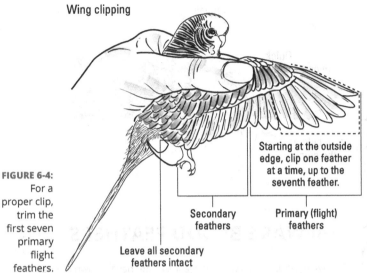

FIGURE 6-4:
For a proper clip, trim the first seven primary flight feathers.

Starting at the outside edge, clip one feather at a time, up to the seventh feather.

Secondary feathers

Primary (flight) feathers

Leave all secondary feathers intact

TIP

Your parakeet's nail has two parts, just like your nails do — the dead part of the nail (on the end), and the *quick,* where the blood supply is. Only cut the dead part of the nail, never the quick. Avoiding the quick is easy when you have a parakeet with light-colored nails — you'll be able to see the vein in the nail and avoid it. If you have a bird with dark-colored nails, trim only a very tiny amount off the tip of the nail, rather than risk hurting your bird.

Again, as with wing trimming, you'll have to gather your parakeet up in a hand towel and make sure not to hold too tightly. A human nail trimmer works well for your parakeet's little nails, or you can use small dog/cat nail trimmers with a round opening at the clipping end. Keep styptic powder on hand at all times in case of bleeding.

TIP

If you make a few passes at your parakeet's nails with a file once a week, the nails will remain trim and you'll eliminate the chances of hurting your bird. Just don't file too much.

REMEMBER

With both nails and wings, you're better off clipping less than more — you can always go back and clip more, but you can't take away the fact that you've cut into a blood feather or the quick of a nail (see Figure 6-5).

I like to clip one nail a day. Parakeets have four toes on each foot, so if you clip just one a day, you'll get them all done in eight days and it will be less traumatic for your bird.

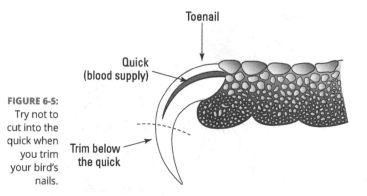

Toenail

Quick
(blood supply)

FIGURE 6-5:
Try not to
cut into the
quick when
you trim
your bird's
nails.

Trim below
the quick

WARNING

BEWARE BLOOD FEATHERS

Blood feathers, also called *pin feathers,* are newly grown feathers that still have a blood supply and will bleed if they're cut or broken. You can recognize blood feathers by the sheath of material encasing them. If your parakeet is light in color, you may even be able to see a vein inside the feather.

Under no circumstances should you ever cut a blood feather, but if you do, you may have to pull the feather out to stop the bleeding. This advice sounds brutal, I know, but it's actually a commonly practiced method of dealing with broken blood feathers. Simply hold the wing firmly and pull the feather *straight out* with a pair of strong tweezers, *hemostats* (a medical tool used to clamp blood vessels and other things), or small pliers. Do *not* pull the feather out at an angle. Pull swiftly, but don't yank. If done incorrectly, you can actually pull out a chunk of flesh and hurt the bird.

If you're too queasy to pull out the broken or cut blood feather yourself, and I don't blame you if you are, rush to the veterinarian after you've applied a clotting agent to the bleeding area. Even if you've pulled the blood feather yourself, visiting a veterinarian after you've done so is a good idea, just to make sure your bird has no further injury.

Chapter **7**

Come Here Often? Getting to Know Your Parakeet

O ne reason why the parakeet has become the world's favorite bird is because of its behavior. The parakeet is a bundle of energy, affectionate and saucy, talkative, and is, in general, pretty predictable. This chapter helps you recognize normal, unusual, and abnormal parakeet behavior.

Understanding Parakeet Behavior

Each bird has its own personality, likes, and dislikes, but some behaviors are common to all parakeets. These behaviors include:

» **Dancing in front of the cage door.** *Translation:* "Get me outta here!" A parakeet making a commotion in front of the cage door wants to come out and play.

- >> **Head tipped downward, as if in prayer.** *Translation:* "Gimme a little head scratch!" When you're playing with your parakeet and it tips its head toward you, it wants a little gentle preening.

- >> **Backing into a corner, beak open, wings flared.** *Translation:* "Stay back!" This bird is being territorial at the moment. It may also be frightened.

- >> **Crouched posture, wings fluttering, staring at you.** *Translation:* "Play with me — now!" This posture (see Figure 7-1), especially with the wings fluttering, means that your little bird is really in love with you!

- >> **Fluffing and shaking.** *Translation:* "I'm sleepy" or "I'm getting ready to do something other than what I'm doing right now." A sleepy parakeet will fluff and shake its feathers a few times before drifting off to sleep. You can liken this to a human tossing and turning a few times before getting completely comfortable. A quick fluff and shake means that the bird is about to embark on a new task.

- >> **Beak tapping (between two birds).** *Translation:* Parakeets tap their beaks together when doing a mating dance. This shows their interest in each other. Sometimes a single bird will beak tap its favorite toys in lieu of having another bird around.

FIGURE 7-1:
A parakeet in a crouched position like this is generally ready to go somewhere.

>> **Banging toys around.** *Translation:* "I'm sick of being in this cage" or "I'm having amorous feelings that I need to express." Parakeets bang their toys around for many reasons, but these are the most common. The bird could also just be playing.

In the following sections, I cover many of the behaviors you may see in your parakeet. All these behaviors are completely normal.

Cleaning and grinding the beak

Your parakeet will likely wipe its beak after it eats, and may rake its beak across the bars of the cage or on toys. The bird is just keeping itself clean. A healthy parakeet will also grind the upper and lower parts of its beak together after eating or before falling asleep. This behavior is a tension-reliever for a bird. This grinding isn't meant to trim the beak — it's more a measure of contentment.

Preening

A healthy bird will sort through its feathers with its beak, making sure they're all in order, cleaning the unruly and ruffled feathers of debris, and creating a neat and orderly appearance. This behavior is known as *preening*.

WARNING

If your parakeet *isn't* preening, it's probably ill. Make an appointment with your avian vet to have the bird examined. If you notice that your parakeet has become ragged and disheveled looking, with debris attached to its feathers or patches of feathers missing, get it some medical attention right away.

Parakeets in pairs will engage in mutual preening, called *allopreening*. (See Figure 7-2.) This behavior is convenient for those hard-to-reach places, like the top of the head. It's also part of the bonding process.

FIGURE 7-2:
Parakeets who live together may enjoy mutual preening, called *allopreening.*

Fluffing and shaking the feathers

When your parakeet is getting ready for a catnap or bedtime, it will fluff itself and then shake out its feathers a few times, which helps to release energy and make it comfortable. Parakeets also shake themselves when they get ready to do a new task, such as eat or take a bath, and they always shake after grooming, allowing all the debris they've just picked off to fall away and leave the feathers clean.

WARNING

If you notice that your parakeet remains fluffed and that it's sleeping for hours on end when it used to be playing, the bird may be ill.

Stretching

Your parakeet will perform a kind of daily birdy yoga, stretching all parts of its body. You bird will amaze you with the kinds of stretches it can do. He'll lift a leg and wing, both on the same side at the same time, and do a long, satisfying stretch. This type of stretch is called *mantling.*

Yawning and sneezing

Parakeets yawn and sneeze just as people do. Parakeets yawn for much the same reasons as well, and they pass a yawn onto their pals, just as humans do, too. Parakeets sneeze to clear their nasal passages when they're clogged. Sound familiar? But frequent sneezing or inflamed nostrils along with sneezing can indicate illness.

Resting on one leg

Your healthy parakeet will often sleep or rest on one leg, which helps to regulate its body temperature.

WARNING

If you notice that your parakeet is sleeping with both feet on the perch, fluffed up, with its head tucked behind it, your bird may be ill. Watch for other signs of illness and get your bird some medical attention if the behavior continues.

Tucking and bobbing the head

Your parakeet will likely sleep with its head tucked in the fluffed up feathers on its back. Although it's completely normal behavior, some birds choose not to sleep this way (just as some people sleep on their sides and others prefer their backs).

Bobbing of the head is normal, too. You'll often see this during feeding behaviors and mating dances.

WARNING

If the bobbing becomes obsessive, it may indicate that a foreign object, such as a small piece of spray millet, is caught in the back of its throat. Yawning along with head-bobbing could indicate an ear infection. If these behaviors continue or if the bobbing produces vomit that crusts on the bird's beak and feathers, call your avian veterinarian.

Scratching

Parakeets are almost constantly moving and preening — scratching is just part of the parakeet routine. Don't be concerned that something is wrong with your bird unless you notice very excessive scratching that results in a lot of feather loss, bleeding, or bald patches.

Scratching can also be caused by the parasite *Giarardia*, which can come from fecal-contaminated water. In addition to itching and self-plucking, symptoms include diarrhea, dehydration, and weight loss.

Regurgitating

Believe it or not, your bird bobbing its head and trying to regurgitate its pre-digested food on you is a sign of intense affection. Regurgitation is how birds feed one another and how they feed their babies. Your parakeet, especially a male, may regurgitate to you, his toys, or his mate. Yes, it's as gross as it sounds, but you should take it as a compliment. Though this behavior is flattering, simply put your bird back into its cage to cool down a bit rather than encouraging it.

If you notice that your bird is sitting on the perch (or the bottom of the cage) vomiting onto its chest and the material is sticking to its feathers and face and the bird is shaking its head to get the vomit off, get veterinary attention right away. No healthy adult parakeet allows debris to accumulate on its feathers.

Regurgitation and vomiting are different. Regurgitation is for affection and to feed mates and babies and vomiting is due to illness.

Flapping the wings

Sometimes a parakeet will stand on a perch and flap its wings vigorously, like birdy calisthenics. If you see your parakeet doing this, don't be alarmed. Your bird is just exercising, getting rid of some of the energy it has built up in its little system. Even if your parakeet has a very large cage, such as an aviary, it may still flap to its heart's content. Parakeets also flap to loosen their feathers during a molt and help speed up the process of growing new feathers.

Playing

Playing comes in many forms, such as chewing, banging toys around, chasing cage mates, zooming around the aviary, tossing food out of the bowl, anything to remain entertained. Sometimes what looks like aggression, such as violently banging a certain toy against the cage, is just a form of play and is nothing to be concerned about.

Dancing on the perch

Male parakeets do a funny thing I like to call "perch dancing." the male struts up and down the perch, bobbing his head, dilating his pupils, and chattering. This dance is intended to get the attention of the female, who generally sits there, pretending not to notice. It's a charming little dance, and it's perfectly normal. Your male parakeet may dance to a toy, or even to you if you're lucky.

Getting excited

Parakeet excitement comes in many forms, such as clambering around the cage, flying, making loud noises, and talking, among others. Sometimes parakeets are excited by certain types of music or by the addition of something new in the home.

Normal parakeet vocalizations

It is said that beauty is in the eye of the beholder. Well, noise is in the ear of the listener. Parakeets aren't known to be loud birds, but some people might be sensitive to their noise.

Parakeets vocalize most in the mornings (either at dawn or whenever you turn on the lights or uncover the cage) and at dusk. During the day, there may be periods of quiet, but for the most part parakeets are lively and chatty. Here are some of their more common vocalizations:

>> **Chittering or chattering:** A happy parakeet will chatter for a good part of the day. This is a happy sound.

>> **Contact calls:** Parakeet pairs will call to each other to check in and make sure that the other is nearby if they are out of sight. If you have a single parakeet, it may contact call to you if you are bonded. This sounds like a sharp chirrup and will persist until you either call back (you can

just say "I'm here, Sweetie," but use your bird's name) or walk into the room where your bird can see you.

>> **Whistling:** Parakeets learn to whistle very well and may whistle instead of talk.

>> **Talking:** If you're a good teacher, your parakeet will learn to repeat words and phrases. Some parakeets are extremely good talkers and can out talk many of the larger parrots.

>> **Chatting in their sleep:** During the day, many parakeets will chatter in their sleep. This is for a good reason. A napping budgie that's chattering will seem like it's awake to predators, who might think twice about making a meal out of it. Parakeets will not chatter at night in their sleep because that can give away their location to a predator.

Getting scared

Parakeets are prey animals, so they're always on the lookout for something that can harm them. They can perceive threats that aren't actually threatening, such as a birthday balloon, new LED lights, a new piece of furniture or lighting fixture, a new toy, or a new person in the home.

A frightened parakeet may thrash around in its cage, crouch in the corner with the beak wide open, try to bite (or actually bite), or fly aimlessly around, hitting things in the aviary or home. It may stand tall on a perch, making itself very sleek, and look around agitatedly.

TIP

If your bird suddenly starts behaving afraid, look around its environment to see if anything has changed; you might find the source of the fear. If you recently changed the position of the cage, can your bird see anything scary through a window, such as a neighborhood cat or headlights flashing through the window at night?

TIP

To calm a frightened parakeet, remove the offending item (if you know what it is) and cover the cage for half an hour. This should give the bird time to calm down and assess the situation. Your bird is familiar with the comfort of its cage. After half an hour, you can uncover the front of the cage and give it a millet spray. When the bird has eaten for a while, slowly remove the entire cover and the bird should be okay.

Egg laying

Sometime single female parakeets will lay eggs, even without a male around, especially if you've added a nest-like item to the bird's cage, such as a hut or a coconut shell. When the hours of light get longer than the hours of darkness, parakeets will get into breeding mode, often causing the female to lay eggs. This generally happens in the spring or if you leave her light on for more than 12 hours per day. The perception of springtime prompts breeding hormones in both sexes. See Chapter 10 for more on breeding and preventing breeding.

Recognizing Problem Behaviors

Problem behaviors are any behaviors that aren't normal in a healthy, well-cared for parakeet. Look out for these behaviors because they may indicate illness or unhappiness:

>> **Feather plucking:** Most parakeets will not pluck their feathers the way other, larger parrots do, but self-mutilation is not unheard of in parakeets, especially if a medical condition is affecting the bird. Sometimes, an infection or virus can cause an itchy or painful spot that the bird will pick and make bald and raw.

WARNING

If you notice that your parakeet is "over-preening," or you see bald spots on your bird, take it to your avian veterinarian right away, as there could be a serious underlying cause. If there is a sudden dramatic loss of feathers without any regrowth as expected, call your avian veterinarian.

>> **Night frights:** Night frights happen when a parakeet becomes agitated or fearful in the dark and thrashes against the bars of its cage, often causing eye, foot, and feather injury. If you hear thrashing in the night, consider using a nightlight in your parakeet's room or lifting a corner

of the cover during the night so that a bit of light gets through.

>> **Excessive noise and screaming:** Parakeets aren't known for screeching like many of the larger parrots, but they can scream when frightened or unhappy. If your parakeet is screaming, you must investigate right away. It may be caught dangerously on a toy or other birds in the cage might be bullying it.

A screaming or screeching parakeet might also be responding to something new in its environment or perhaps something it sees or hears outside, such as other birds.

If your bird is noisier than usual, it maybe hormonal and in breeding mode. You can try covering the cage, but don't cover the cage as punishment or for an excessive amount of time.

Putting Your Parakeet to Bed

Parakeets need their rest as much as you do. A dark room with a nightlight nearby is good sleeping environment for a parakeet. You can also cover your bird if the room where you keep it tends to be light in the evening or is the room where you watch TV in the evening.

A healthy parakeet typically sleeps with one leg pulled up into its body, making it seem like the bird only has one leg. It may also tuck its head into its fluffed feathers on its back. (See Figure 7-3.)

To put your parakeet to bed, you can just turn out the lights and go to sleep. If you follow this approach, you can expect your bird to go to sleep too if the room is dark and relatively quiet. If there's a lot of light coming from another room, it may keep the bird up and it may chatter for part of the night. If the room has windows without blackout curtains, the birds will definitely wake up with the sun and begin to vocalize.

FIGURE 7-3: Parakeets often sleep with their head tucked backwards.

Many people choose to cover their parakeets at night, which has its advantages. For one, a covered parakeet won't wake up so early in the morning and start chirping. A cover also shuts drafts out of the cage and prevents the birds from disturbances in the night, such as the family cat lurking nearby or a flickering television or computer screen. Covering the cage also prevents drafts and the bird from becoming too chilled. (See Figure 7-4.)

WARNING

Some parakeets don't like being covered and will thrash around at night. If this is the case, cover only three sides of the cage, giving your bird the opportunity to view the rest of the room.

FIGURE 7-4: A parakeet puffed up like this might be feeling chilled.

TIP

If the room where your parakeets are housed is very dark, consider a nightlight. Parakeets can become distraught in the darkness if they hear a noise or feel something moving nearby. Your bird will be better off if it can see that the danger is simply someone getting up for a midnight snack or checking their Insta.

3

Training and Breeding Your Parakeet

Chapter **8**

Good Bird! Taming and Training Your Parakeet

Sometimes people keep parakeets in pairs or in a flock to watch them interact and listen to their pretty chattering. Others want to have a hands-on companion to hold and ride around on their shoulder. (See Figure 8-1.) No matter your preference, this chapter helps you make good friends with your parakeet and introduces you to some fun advanced training techniques.

FIGURE 8-1: This parakeet is being hand-tamed by its human companion.

Handling Your Parakeet Safely

TIP

Parakeets should be handled gently and with respect. Here are some basic ground rules to share with your children when you first bring your parakeet home. *Remember:* These rules also apply to adults. In fact, think of them as ground rules that everyone should follow:

» **Move slowly.** Birds are frightened by quick movements. Explain to children that the bird won't hurt them (not badly, anyway) and that it's important to remain calm, no matter what happens.

» **Speak softly.** Loud noises are terrifying to a parakeet. Use a soft, soothing voice when talking to the bird.

» **Don't fear the bird.** Fear of the new parakeet will lead to an unhappy and neglected bird.

» **Never shake, hit, or rattle the cage.** A parakeet is going to be only as entertaining as it can be. Children don't always understand this and they try to get the bird to do something more interesting. Explain to children that birds become frightened when their homes are rattled.

» **Allow the bird to play.** Birds need some out-of-cage time every day. With your busy life, you can easily forget that your bird relies on you for interaction. Perhaps the bird can sit on your shoulder while you browse social media on your phone, do homework, or watch TV.

>> **Give the bird a routine.** Birds like to know what will happen and when it will happen. They're control freaks with feathers. Create a parakeet routine for yourself or your child and make sure that you stick with it.

>> **Birds need "time out" too.** Parakeets can get overstimulated and tired if they're handled by an active child (or adult) for hours on end. The poor bird will want nothing more than to take a drink of water, eat a snack, and take a nap. The bird needs a break every half hour or so.

>> **Never take the parakeet outside.** Kids may want to show off their bird to friends, and though that's a valid response to owning this terrific animal, many dangers lurk outside, including the bird flying away. Even a clipped bird can be carried away by a breeze.

>> **Don't squeeze!** Birds are unable to breathe when held, even lightly, around their chest area. Don't "carry around" the bird. Instead, let the bird perch on your hand or shoulder.

REMEMBER

Always supervise your child's playtime with your parakeet. Children are whimsical and may leave the bird somewhere or may become panicked by a little nip. A good tip is to place a square of painter's tape on the floor around your bird's cage and then tell the children in the house that they aren't to go inside the tape square. This may help to keep them from putting their little fingers into the cage.

Taming Your Parakeet

Most people will not spend countless hours training their parakeets to perform elaborate behaviors, but if you put in the time, it's very possible for your parakeet to learn some amazing things. Most people simply want their parakeet to be friendly, not bite, and to enjoy the company of humans, so I'll focus on taming in this next section.

Helping your parakeet feel comfortable around you

Handfed baby parakeets are not easy to find in the general pet marketplace. You can search online to find a breeder in your area that will handfeed a baby for you, or you can purchase a pair, breed them, and handfeed the babies yourself (more on that in Chapter 10).

Most parakeets in the pet shop are four months to a year old, but you will be unlikely to know any bird's exact age. Unless you've bought a handfed baby, you can't just fish a parakeet out of its cage, place it on your finger, and expect it to stay there. The untamed parakeet will flutter or fly as far away from you as possible and go to the highest point it can reach.

TIP

If you have a skittish young bird, begin the taming process about a week to ten days after you bring your new bird home. You have to give your parakeet some time to get acclimated to its new environment, so you don't want to start on the very first day.

TIP

You can do several things to make this taming time comfortable for your bird:

>> Talk in a soothing tone to your new bird, saying its name over and over.

>> Offer treats, such as millet spray, placing them inside the cage and letting your hand linger inside for a moment.

>> Place your hand on the side of the cage, very slowly, two or three times a day. Don't expect the bird to come near you. You're just trying to get your new bird used to your hand being nearby.

TIP

During the taming phase, play hide-and-seek with your parakeet. Hide around a corner and whistle and click to your bird to get it interested in what you're doing. When your bird whistles or vocalizes back, pop out and greet it in an excited tone.

Talk and sing as much as you can around your parakeet, especially when you're servicing its cage. The bird will get used to the sound of your voice and it may even begin calling to you for more vocal interaction.

The key to taming and training a parakeet is trust. Making taming and training fun is the best way to gain your bird's trust. Keeping that in mind, here are some taming and training don'ts:

>> Don't grab a frightened and thrashing bird out of the cage and whisk its away to another room — you'll just end up scaring your bird even more.

>> Never, ever wear gloves during taming or training. Gloves will only terrify your parakeet and it won't get used to the human hand.

>> Don't yell at or hit your parakeet, ever, ever, *ever*. Those are just not good training tactics (and are considered animal abuse).

>> Don't get your feelings hurt by a bite — your bird isn't being a jerk; it's just being a bird. **Remember:** The more reaction you have when the bird bites you, the more frequently and harder the bird is likely to bite. If you're calm and behave as if the bite doesn't hurt at all, the bird will be less likely to bite next time.

The first thing you have to do is build trust with your bird, making each hands-on experience with your parakeet a pleasant one. If each time you play with your parakeet you behave in a mature, soothing manner, making yourself a fun and enjoyable companion, you and your parakeet will have a great relationship for many years. (See Figure 8-2.)

Before you try to tame your parakeet, you need have an avian veterinarian or bird groomer clip its wings so that it can't fly away into a wall or mirror, which can be disastrous. Don't worry, the wing feathers grow back. Even if you eventually want your parakeet to be a "flyer," you won't get far in your training if you have an unclipped bird. Your parakeet will easily be able to get away from you if it can fly, and that doesn't do much for the training process.

Showing your bird how to trust you

TIP

After your bird is comfortable around you, you can start trying to train your parakeet. Just keep these suggestions in mind:

>> Bribe the parakeet with fun foods and toys it likes.

>> Move slowly and talk in a soothing manner.

>> Try to read your parakeet's body language. If the bird is getting increasingly terrified or frustrated, put it back into its cage for a rest.

>> Do several short training sessions a day rather than one or two long ones. Shoot for no longer than 10 or 15 minutes.

>> Have realistic expectations for your parakeet. Training takes time.

Most parakeets love millet spray. Reserve millet spray for training sessions (you can offer it in the cage when the bird is tamed). Begin by placing the spray of millet in your hand and encouraging your bird to eat from your hand. Most parakeets will happily accept millet from you and might even jump onto your hand to eat it. Success!

An easy behavior to train your parakeet to do is the step-up. *Step-up* is when your bird steps gently on to your hand or finger.

Fortunately, your finger is kind of like a perch, and if your finger is always steady and safe, your parakeet will eventually learn to trust you.

Parakeets are fast learners — especially with simple tasks, like step-up. All it takes to teach a parakeet anything is mutual trust and patience. Using a gentle, slow training method is preferable with animals as sensitive as parakeets.

Begin by allowing the bird to come out of its cage by itself. Try not to frighten the bird. Place a perch on top of its cage, or let it climb on to a standing perch where it will be standing on a dowel, not a flat surface. If your parakeet is a tame youngster, you can gently lift it out of the cage, being careful that you don't hurt its feet as it grasps onto the bars or a perch.

Take the bird to a small room, perhaps a closet or a bathroom, but definitely a place that's parakeet-proofed so that it doesn't get hurt. If you're taking it to the bathroom, put the toilet lid down and remove any cleaning products. (You want to parakeet-proof the room *before* you take the bird out of the cage.)

After you're in the small room, sit down with your knees bent and up. Place the bird on one knee. The idea is to have it stay there so that you can talk to it and offer millet spray as a snack, all the while creeping your hand slowly up your leg toward it. In your first few sessions, it will probably fly off. That's okay — just pick it up and place it back onto your knee.

When you have its trust (after a few sessions) and after the bird has let you get very close with your hand, try to rub its chest and belly softly and gently with the length of your index finger, cooing to it, pushing on its belly, and slowly increasing the pressure.

Increase the pressure on its belly a little more, and your bird will lift up a foot to keep its balance. Place your finger under its lifted foot and lift the bird, if it allows. If not, simply allow its foot to remain on your hand until the bird removes it. As you do this, tell the bird clearly to *step up*. Many parakeets will say "step up" and wave one foot in the air when they want you to pick them up. This cue becomes a great communication tool.

When your bird is fairly good at stepping up, you can have it step from finger to finger, repeating the phrase "step up" and praising it.

Talking to Your Parakeet — and Getting It to Talk to You

Parakeets are among the best talking birds, able to mimic hundreds of words and phrases. Both males and females are able to talk, and some individuals are very chatty, whereas others won't talk much at all. Whistling is easier for a parakeet to learn, so if you teach whistles before you teach talking, your bird may prefer the whistling and may not talk much. But each parakeet is different in this regard.

The best (and only) way to teach any bird to talk is through repetition. Your bird will say the things that you say all the time. If you want, you can make a recording and play it when you're not home. But your parakeet is more likely to learn things that you say in person. It's paying attention to its human family and trying to get their attention and be part of the household by talking.

Some people use baby talk when they talk to their parakeets and others talk to them like they are adult humans. Talk to your parakeets whichever way feels natural to you, but realize that you have to speak very clearly if you want your bird to speak clearly as well.

Repeating yourself a lot is the best way to get your bird to say what you want it to say. Most people don't need to make this much effort — a parakeet generally repeats what it hears a lot, usually its name and *hello*. A parakeet will generally also repeat what it hears you saying to other people in the house. If you have naughty kids, your bird may learn to say, "I told you to stop hitting your sister!"

Try to teach your parakeet your name and phone number in case it ever gets lost. Many people do this, and it actually does work to return the bird to its family. Simply repeat your name and phone number over and over — you can make a little song of it if you'd like — and the bird may very well pick it up.

Dealing with Biting

A nip from a parakeet isn't terrible, but it can hurt depending on where on your hand the nip occurs. First, you need to know the difference between an actual bite and your bird just being playful. A bite or nip happens mostly when it's fearful, hormonal, molting, or tired and cranky. A playful "bite" or nibble happens when your bird is exploring your hand, ear, arm, or face — whatever part of your body it is near. It usually doesn't hurt.

If your bird bites you out of fear during the training process, don't yell, hit, fling the bird or spray water on it — please! Very calmly say "no bite," wait a few moments, then offer some millet or seeds to show, once again, that you are a safe, fun person to be around. You *must* put a few moments in-between the bite and the treat or your bird will think that you are rewarding the bite, which is not your goal in training.

WARNING

Some people use the "wobble method" of dealing with biting. You need very good timing to use this method. When your parakeet is biting you (this can only work as the bite is occurring) you will wobble your hand a little to set the bird off balance. This will cause it to cease the bite to try to regain balance. You have to be careful using this method. First, you want your parakeet to trust that your hand is a solid, safe place to perch, so if you wobble too much, that can be scary and your bird won't feel safe perching on you. Second, your bird is small and fragile, so too big of a wobble could frighten it off of your hand and onto the hard floor or cause it to fly into a solid object. You can wobble a little, just to set your bird slightly off balance, but don't do it roughly or often.

Most people pull back instinctively when a bird bites. Rather than pulling your hand away, *gently* push in toward the bite. This will set your bird off balance and he will likely let go. Fortunately, parakeets don't bite and hang on like some other birds. A bite is usually pretty quick.

If you are being bitten out of fear a lot, step back your training process to whatever you were doing before your bird started biting you. Fill your hand with seeds and place it slowly into the cage and see if you can get your bird to eat from your hand. That's great progress!

TIP

Punishment doesn't work on birds, so you can't punish a bite. Biting actually doesn't occur in the wild. It's a behavior that captive birds learn out of necessity. Bird behavior is counterintuitive for humans. For example, you can't give your bird a time-out the way you would a toddler. If you put your bird back into its cage every time it bites you, it will learn that it only has to bite you to go back to where it feels safe and where you won't bother it.

Instead of allowing a bite to frazzle you, continue your training session until one good thing happens, such as the bird eating out of your hand or perching on your finger. After this one success, you can then take your bird back to its cage or playpen. In fact, you should always end each training session on a high note.

If you are being bitten because your bird is tired and wants to go back to its housing, is molting and cranky, or it is having seasonal hormonal crankiness, just give your bird some space and try again later. Remember that everyone — including your bird — is allowed to have its feelings.

Finding Fun in Potty Training

There are two ways to potty train a bird. The first way is to teach your bird that you will only remove it from the cage after it has pooped. The second is to remove your bird from the cage and then give a verbal cue for your bird to poop into a trash can or onto a paper plate or napkin. I'm not a fan of the second method because your bird might learn to hold in its poop and can make itself sick, so let's talk about the first method.

Get to know your bird's "poop cues." A parakeet that's about to poop will back up a little on the perch, squat a little, raise its tail, and then its bombs away.

Instead of creating a verbal cue (like "go poop") to teach your bird to poop on command, which can become unhealthy, reward your bird for pooping in its cage or onto its playpen before you pick it up. This is easy. Stand at the cage or playpen and wait for your bird to poop. Say "good poop" and then pick up your bird (this training only works with hand-tame birds). Now offer a treat.

Ideally, your bird will come to associate you picking it up (which presumably it wants) with having just pooped and will poop as you approach the cage.

Parakeets poop several times an hour. Poop happens. You're going to get pooped on. You're going to find poop in the strangest places. No method of potty training is going to make that stop. Fortunately, parakeet poop doesn't smell, won't stain clothes, and isn't harmful to you at all unless you allow it to cake onto the cage and dry, which will then become powder that you can breathe.

TIP Wear an old, knit, button-down shirt when you play with your parakeets (knit stretches and is easy to stand on, whereas woven fabrics don't stretch and can be slippery). You may need a couple. These are your parakeet playtime shirts that you are sacrificing to the poop gods.

TIP Bird poop is easier to clean when it's dry. If you find a squiggle of poop on your shirt or a piece of furniture, simply wait for it to dry and then pick it off. If you try to clean a poop while it's wet, you may end up smearing it. Yuck.

Learning Advanced Training Techniques

With time and a lot of patience, you can teach your parakeet to do some remarkable things. I'm not talking about tricks, I'm talking about real learning, real communication. Read on to discover some truly remarkable behaviors you can teach your bird.

What is advanced training?

Advanced training opens up the lines of communication between you and your bird. I'd like to introduce you to the work of Jennifer Cunha, an animal cognition trainer and attorney from Florida. She is doing some of the most intriguing and advanced work with parrot cognition today. Her parrots can tell her what they want, identify colors, count, write, color, and so much more.

Typically, these types of training methods are used with much larger parrots, but parakeets are intelligent enough to learn some of them. I'll offer you three of Jennifer's basic methods here, but if you want to know more, please visit https:// parrotkindergarten.com.

Preference training

Preference training opens up a world of communication for your parakeet. You and your bird don't need any prior training experience to do this. With preference training, your bird will learn to tell you what it prefers between two offered items.

Here are some easy steps to begin preference training:

1. **Take two of your parakeet's regular treats and hold one in each hand.**

   For example, Jennifer starts with a pine nut and a sunflower seed. For a parakeet, you may want to use a tiny bit of millet spray and a small sunflower seed.

2. **Show your bird the two items, say what they are, and then ask, "which is favorite?"**

   Your bird will reach for one of the treats, which you then give to it.

3. **Swap the treats in your hands to make sure that your parakeet isn't just choosing the same side rather than choosing the treat it likes the best and ask again, "Which is favorite?" and wait for your bird to choose.**

4. **Again swap the treats from hand to hand and repeat.**

   Sometimes, keep the treats in the same hand. Your parakeet will most likely continue to choose its favorite of the two items. Consistency is the best signal to knowing whether your bird is actually choosing a favorite item or just reaching for whatever is closest. Three out of three, or at least two out of three, is ideal, and it may take a few sessions for your bird to learn this communication skill. Patience is important!

TIP

If your parakeet is skittish, you can teach preference training by letting your parakeet simply look at both options, and whichever one it looks at longer — for at least a period of two to three seconds — is the one you can drop into a bowl next to it.

After your parakeet understands that the option it touches (or looks at) is what is given to it, you can expand the communication system to discover many of your parakeet's favorite things, such as toys, activities, people, and food and beverages.

Color training

Jennifer says that teaching colors is a fun way to help your bird learn how to learn (and I say that this skill will definitely impress your friends, neighbors, and TikTok!). You can use foam letters as your color training targets. Or, if you choose, you can use plastic toy discs, colored cards, or parrot-safe wood blocks. Whatever you decide, just keep your material consistent when training colors (for example, using all discs or all wood blocks).

Here are the steps to get started teaching colors:

1. Start with red and blue.

   a. Hold up your red item and ask your bird to "touch red." When it touches the red item, say, "Good," and offer a small morsel of her favorite treat, like a piece of millet. Repeat this several times.

   b. Remove the red item and move to the blue item. Ask your bird to "touch blue." Repeat the same procedure as with the red item. When the bird touches the blue item after you've asked, say, "Good," and then treat.

   For some birds, simply playing with the target is enough for a reward, but many birds will train better with a treat given to them or dropped in their food bowl.

2. Hold up both the red and blue items and say, "Touch red."

   a. When your parakeet touches the red item, say, "Good," and treat.

   b. Do the same for blue. Repeat red and blue touch training again with the objects in the same hands.

c. *Swap hands and ask your bird to touch the red, and then ask it to touch the blue.*

TIP

If your bird gets it wrong when you're holding up both the red and the blue items twice in a row, remove one and go back to asking just for the touch (or look) for one color. Give your bird the chance to succeed. Try not to allow your bird to get more than two questions wrong in a row before going back to the initial teaching phase of this concept.

Aim for three out of four correct questions in a row, or 75 percent accuracy in a session. You bird doesn't need to be perfect. After your bird is showing some consistency with the correct answer, teach new colors so she doesn't get bored.

Teaching yes and no

Yes and *no* are fairly advanced concepts for any organism. According to Jennifer, teaching your parakeet to understand and use yes and no opens up a whole world of possibilities for it. Your bird can tell you what it wants and doesn't want. Learning yes and no for any parrot breaks a huge communication barrier. Here's how to get started.

To start yes/no training, try these steps:

1. **Choose a red and green foam toy object, or the same objects such as wood blocks or plastic toy discs in those two different colors.**

   Red is typically associated with no and green with yes, so assign those values to the colored objects. You can also write the words "yes" and "no" on a card if that's easier for you, however, many birds can learn that the same items have different properties.

2. **Starting with the green object, show your parakeet the object and ask your bird to "touch yes."**

   When it does, say "Good" and offer a treat. Repeat four times. Do the same for the red "no" object.

3. **Hold both objects up and say, "Touch yes."**

Ideally, your parakeet will choose the object you've assigned as yes. If not, ask again. If it fails a third time, go back to Step 1. After your bird selects the yes object on cue while you are holding both objects, ask it to touch no and repeat the training. Your bird should eventually be able to choose the correctly named object.

4. **Swap hands to ensure that your bird truly understands what you're teaching.**

Your parakeet won't understand what yes and no mean at this point. It will simply associate the two different words with the objects.

5. **Build on this skill by teaching some vocabulary, in this case, the word "treat" by holding up a treat and say, "Touch treat."**

Of course, your bird will reach for the treat. Say "Good," give it the treat, hold up another treat, and say again, "Touch treat." Repeat four to seven times until your bird is successful every time.

6. **Hold up a bowl of water and say, "Touch water."**

You bird may or may not want the water. If it touches the water, say, "Good," and offer a treat. If it doesn't touch the water, but gets close enough to it, that's fine. You can still praise and treat. Typically, parakeets will want the treats more than they want the water.

7. **Hold up your yes and no objects and ask, "Would you like a treat?"**

If your bird touches the yes target, say yes and offer a treat. If it touches the no target, say, "Okay, no treat," and ask again. If your bird chooses no twice in a row, only offer the yes object and repeat this step several times. Then offer the yes and no objects again, and ask, "Do you want a treat?"

Suddenly, the green yes target means the bird gets a treat when asked if it wants a treat and the red no target means no treat. When your bird chooses "yes," it learns that it gets the item offered.

8. **Show the yes and no targets and ask, "Do you want some water?"**

If yes, offer water. Typically, the bird won't want the water if it isn't thirsty. Put the water down and ask again. If the bird chooses yes for the water again, offer water again. Eventually, it will learn to say no to the water if it wants the treat more. When it chooses the no target when offered water, don't offer the water but do offer a treat, because that answer was correct. Now switch the targets to the opposite hands and repeat the process to ensure that your bird truly understands what the targets mean.

Chapter 9

Keeping Your Parakeet Healthy and Handling Emergencies

The best defense for a parakeet against illness is a diligent guardian. Just like you, your parakeet needs a doctor and yearly check-ups. Your bird also needs you to know when it's not feeling well, which means you need to understand the signs of avian illness and injury. Finally, in the rare event of a parakeet emergency, your bird needs you to find the help it needs — and fast! This chapter helps you to become your parakeet's first line of defense.

Finding a Veterinarian

For your parakeet, you want an *avian veterinarian*, a vet who specializes in the care and treatment of birds. They aren't always easy to find! A veterinarian who specializes in fur isn't the same as one who specializes in feathers.

TIP

The best place to find an avian vet in your area is by calling the Association of Avian Veterinarians at 720-458-4111 or visiting www.aav.org.

Regular examinations

REMEMBER

Take your new feathered companion to an avian veterinarian within three days of buying it if you can. Here's why:

>> If you bought your parakeet with a health guarantee, you'll have some recourse if tests reveal that your new bird is ill.

>> You'll begin a relationship with the vet, and the vet will get to know your bird and be able to evaluate it better because the doctor will know what your bird is like when he's healthy. This is called *establishing a baseline*.

>> Some avian vets won't take an emergency patient unless the bird is a regular client. You don't want to be stuck without someone to call if your parakeet encounters an emergency.

>> Avian vets often board birds in their offices, though some will only board clients — that way they can be relatively sure that the bird won't bring diseases into their office.

>> You'll get some important recommendations from the doctor, including information on diet and housing.

TIP

Even when your parakeet is well, you should take it to your avian veterinarian once a year. Your veterinarian will run some routine tests and weigh your bird. This *well-bird check-up* will allow your veterinarian to keep records of your healthy bird and will make it easier to determine when it's ill.

Emergencies

When you have an emergency involving your parakeet, you *must* take it to an avian veterinarian right away.

So what qualifies as an emergency? If you have *one single moment* of worry about something that has happened to your bird (it has flown into a window, broken a toe, is bleeding, having trouble breathing, and so on), or if you notice blood in the droppings or a drastic change in your parakeet's behavior, you probably have an emergency.

Don't hesitate to rush your bird to the avian veterinarian. Minutes are crucial in an emergency. *Remember:* Your bird is a small, sensitive creature more likely to be overcome by the stress of an accident than a larger animal.

What a Healthy Bird Looks Like

Knowing something about the parakeet's bodily systems and observing your bird carefully when he's healthy will help you to be able to tell if he's ill.

Eyes

A healthy eye is clear, moist, and free of discharge. A parakeet with an eye problem may squint or scratch it excessively with its foot or will rub its eye on the perch or sides of its cage. Sometimes, thrashing in the cage or fighting with other birds can cause eye injuries.

If you see swollen eyelids, cloudy eyes, excessive blinking or discharge, and tearing, have your bird checked out by your vet.

Ears

Your parakeet's ears are located a short distance parallel from the eyes and look like holes in the head. Each ear opening is covered by feathers. You may get a glimpse of the ear openings after your parakeet bathes, when the feathers around its head are wet and stuck together.

If you can see your parakeet's ear opening clearly without the bird being wet, make an appointment with your avian veterinarian.

TIP

Beak

Your parakeet's beak is made of the same durable material as your fingernails. The beak grows over a basically hollow honeycomb-like structure, a convenient design for an animal that should be light enough to fly. The beak acts as a crushing tool but is delicate enough to peel the skin off a pea. The beak also helps your parakeet around, kind of like another foot.

Your parakeet should be able to keep its beak trim through eating and playing. If your bird's beak is overgrown (see Figure 9-1), it could be an indication of a nutritional disorder, mange, or mites, in which case you'll have to take it to an avian veterinarian for treatment. The beak can also become injured, cracked, or split, any of which requires a veterinary visit.

Never try to trim your parakeet's beak yourself.

WARNING

FIGURE 9-1:
An overgrown beak may be a sign of malnutrition or mites.

The *cere*, the fleshy place just above the beak, can sometimes become thick and rough in *hens* (female birds), a condition called *brown hypertrophy.* This condition, caused by increased hormones, is not dangerous. The increased layering on the cere does not need to be removed.

Feet

In addition to walking and climbing, birds also use their feet to regulate their body temperature. When your parakeet is cold, it may draw one leg up into its body and stand on the other leg. When your parakeet is warm, the blood flow will increase to its legs, which will help its whole body cool down.

Several injuries are common to the feet, including catching toes on cages and toys, as well as problems with the leg band. Swelling in the legs could be a symptom of *gout* (a painful condition that can be the result of poor nutrition). If the skin on the bottom of the foot is red and inflamed, or even scabby, this could be a sign of *bumblefoot* (an infection associated with poor nutrition and obesity).

TIP

If you notice something wrong with your bird's legs or feet, take it to your avian vet. Contact your avian veterinarian right away if you notice any foot or leg weakness or *lameness* (inability to walk).

Feathers

A healthy parakeet should be obsessed with taking care of its feathers, preening them for much of the day. A parakeet likes to keep its feathers neat, clean, and well organized on its body.

Birds *molt* (shed their feathers and grow new ones) once or twice a year, usually during seasonal changes. When your parakeet molts, you'll notice feathers on the bottom of the cage, but you shouldn't be able to see patches of skin on your bird. (If you do notice bald spots, contact your vet — it could indicate a serious medical problem.)

When a new feather begins growing, it will be encased in a protective sheath called a *pin feather*. Pin feathers can be itchy and your parakeet may become cranky at this time.

Respiratory system

Parakeets have a very sensitive respiratory system, which is sensitive to airborne irritants, such as aerosol sprays, fumes from heated nonstick cookware and other surfaces, and smoke. They are prone to respiratory illness and distress because their respiratory system is more complicated than ours.

TIP

If you notice your parakeet panting and it's standing on a perch and its tail is bobbing, call your avian veterinarian and describe the situation. If you notice a drastic change in your bird's breathing or, in extreme cases, bubbling from the mouth or nostrils, take your parakeet to the veterinarian right away.

WARNING

Keep your parakeet away from fumes and airborne toxins. Your bird should not be anywhere near heated non-stick items, scented candles, and aerosol items, such as air fresheners or hair spray. Ventilate very well when using non-stick items or round them all up and take them to the thrift store. I've heard many tragic stories of parakeets dropping dead in another room while someone is cooking in the kitchen with a non-stick pan. See Chapter 4 for a list of the usual household non-stick culprits.

TIP

The one big proactive thing you can do to make sure your parakeet maintains a healthy respiratory system is to allow it to fly. Flying keeps a bird's respiratory system strong.

Skeletal system

Many of your parakeet's bones are filled with air, and all of them are thin-walled, which makes them light enough for flight. Though bird bones are strong enough to allow the movement of wings in flight, they're easily broken.

TIP

If you suspect that one of your parakeet's bones is broken, take it to the veterinarian immediately. Some of the bones contain air sacs that aid in breathing, and your bird may experience respiratory distress if it has broken bones. Symptoms should be relatively obvious — if you see your bird with a leg hanging, a wing hanging, or the bird goes lame (can't walk or perhaps can't even move), it could indicate a break. Of course, if you see a break (as you would in a human), you'll know right away.

Digestive system

The parakeet's digestive system begins with the beak and ends with the vent. After your bird swallows food, the food goes to the *crop* at the top of the bird's breast. From the crop, the food goes to the gizzard, which is the part of the stomach that grinds the food. The food moves on to the *cloaca*, where the feces (the green, sometimes black or dark brown portion of the dropping depending upon what the parakeet eats), encircles the *urates* (the white or cream-colored opaque part of the dropping), and the urine forms a slight clear puddle around both that is collected before being eliminated through the *vent*.

Because your parakeet will probably be munching all day, she'll be pooping all day too. This is normal. Frequent pooping is a function of flying — a bird that's holding a load of poop is going to be heavier, so nature gave birds a smaller area to hold waste, so it has to be eliminated often.

TIP

If you notice a drastic change in your bird's droppings, see your avian veterinarian. A change can mean a different consistency (harder or more liquid than normal), blood in the feces, an extreme color change (yellow, black, red, and so on), and undigested food. Also, if you parakeet's vent becomes caked with droppings, that's generally a sign of a number of serious health problems.

Helping Your Parakeet Get the Exercise It Needs

Wild parakeets fly around all day searching for food and water, and as a result, wild parakeets don't get chunky. The companion parakeet, however, is highly prone to obesity. Exercise is essential to maintain your parakeet's good health, and flying is the absolute best exercise for birds. It's the most natural behavior that they have and gives them a sense of purpose. Some people allow their parakeets to fly around the house (hopefully the house has been parakeet-proofed first). Many people build aviaries (bird housing that is large enough for an adult human to fit inside) where their birds can fly.

REMEMBER

Many dangers lurk in the common household. Flying inside the house may not be the best idea, though some parakeets live out long lives doing just that. For information on parakeet-proofing your home, see Chapter 4.

WARNING

A friendly bird may want to follow you around, sometimes on the floor, and you could accidentally step on it, especially if your bird's coloring is similar to your floor's coloring. A parakeet allowed access to the floor may also become victim to a slamming door or another pet. Keep your parakeet off the floor and you eliminate one of the many dangers that threaten this little bird.

TIP

A good exercise for parakeets is *destruction*. Parakeets like to chew, and the more they chew, the more energy they expend. Find toys that your bird likes to fight with, chew, and shred, like toys made of soft wood and raffia, a fiber often used to make baskets and hats.

Play gyms are another good source of exercise, especially the ones with long ladders attached. Encourage your bird to go up and down the ladder.

REMEMBER

The best exercise for your parakeet is to simply get out of the cage and play with you. The more out-of-cage time that your parakeet has, the more exercise he'll get — and the healthier and happier he'll be.

Cleaning Your Parakeet's Housing

Keeping your parakeet's cage and surrounding area clean goes a long way toward keeping it healthy. Dried bird feces can aerosolize, meaning that it can deteriorate into powder and then go floating into the air where your bird, yourself, your family, and your other pets can breathe it in, which isn't healthy for anyone.

Change the bottom of your bird's cage at least every other day if you can. Once a week, pull out the grate at the bottom of the cage and soak it in a ten-percent bleach/water solution (one part bleach to ten parts water). Make sure to rinse and dry it very well before returning it to the cage.

You can provide your parakeet with a separate, smaller cage while you clean its larger cage, especially if you're using bleach. You can also use baking soda as an abrasive cleaner, which isn't toxic to birds. A vinegar solution in a spray bottle is also a good, non-toxic disinfectant. An effective ratio is a 1:1 solution, one part vinegar to one part water. Add a few teaspoons of fresh lemon juice to make it smell nice.

Signs of a Sick Parakeet

There are dozens of viral, bacterial, fungal, and parasitical infections that can plague your parakeet, too many to detail here. Many of these infections are preventable with good cleanliness, dietary, quarantine, and health practices.

Any odd behavior may indicate illness, but not always. Parakeets, like most birds, are creatures of routine, and a sudden break in routine signals that you should investigate your bird's condition.

TIP

If you can't find a reason for the unusual behavior, start looking for symptoms of illness, including the following:

>> **Fluffiness:** If you notice that your parakeet is overly fluffy, it may be trying to retain heat.

>> **Sleepiness:** A sick parakeet may sleep too much. Sleeping on the bottom of the cage is especially alarming.

>> **Loss of appetite:** If you notice that your bird isn't eating, it could have a serious problem.

>> **Weight loss:** This symptom may indicate a number of illnesses, though it can often be difficult to notice weight loss because if your bird's feathers.

>> **Change in attitude:** If your parakeet seems listless and is not behaving in its usual manner, it may be ill.

>> **Change in feathers:** Lack of grooming and feathers falling out in patches can indicate illness.

>> **Lameness:** If your bird can't use its feet, you can be guaranteed that something is wrong. Take your bird to the vet right away.

>> **Panting or labored breathing:** Either of these symptoms can indicate a respiratory ailment, or perhaps overheating. Changes in your parakeet's breathing, changes in vocalization, tail bobbing when breathing, or gasping or wheezing can indicate an infection or an airborne irritant. Panting may also be a sign of egg binding in a female parakeet (see the "Egg binding" section later in this chapter).

>> **Tail bobbing:** If your parakeet is standing straight up on the perch and its tail is noticeably bobbing toward and away from it, your bird may have a respiratory problem, or it may just be out of breath from exercise.

>> **Listlessness:** A formerly active parakeet who has become listless and uninterested in life may be ill.

>> **Discharge:** If you notice any runniness or discharge on the eyes, nostrils, or vent, go to the veterinarian immediately.

>> **Food stuck to the feathers around the face:** This indicates poor grooming or vomiting, and both are possible signs of illness.

>> **Tumors:** Obese parakeets often develop fatty tumors, which may go away with exercise, or may need surgery. Tumors can cause the skin to ulcerate and bleed, and will greatly reduce your parakeet's lifespan.

>> **Change in beak appearance:** A change in the appearance of the beak can indicant scaly-face mites. These occur in young parakeets and older birds with compromised immune systems. These mites cause a crusty appearance on the bird's face and legs, and can result in an overgrown beak. They are easy to treat, but take multiple treatments. Scaly-face mites are not very contagious, but can be passed from bird to bird, so keep infected birds away from others.

>> **Sticky substance in mouth or white mouth lesions:** This can be a sign of a yeast infection, which can affect the mouth and digestive tract, as well as the respiratory

system. Your parakeet normally has a certain amount of yeast in its body, but when its bodily balance is out a whack, when it is undernourished or after a treatment of antibiotics, the fungus can grow to excess. Regurgitation and digestive problems may also occur. Even though this condition is not immediately serious, it can cause death if left untreated.

>> **Abnormal feather growth or feather loss:** If you notice changes in your parakeet's feathers, beyond the normal molting, consult your veterinarian. It may be a symptom of a serious disease, such as psittacine beak and feather disease (PBFD), that may be contagious to your other birds and could result in death.

>> **Drastic change in droppings:** Your parakeet's droppings should consist of a solid green portion, white urates (surrounded by the green), and a clear liquid encircling both. If any of these are discolored (darker green, black, yellow, or red) and there has been no change in diet, your bird may have a serious problem. Red blood found in the droppings always constitutes a critical emergency.

Emergencies: Knowing When to Get Help Immediately

The average home offers plenty of dangers for a parakeet. Even the most careful of owners may encounter an accident with their birds.

WARNING

When an accident happens, the first thing to do is contact your avian veterinarian. *Never* underestimate an emergency. If you notice weakness, a fluffed appearance, quick breathing, droopy eyes, the inability to perch, or your bird lying on the floor of the cage, or bleeding, rush your parakeet to the veterinarian right away.

In the following sections, I cover the more common emergencies. *Remember:* This list doesn't include everything that could happen to your bird, so if you notice something that doesn't seem quite right, don't hesitate to take your bird to the vet and have it examined.

Poisoning

Poisoning generally happens when a parakeet gets into a household product. Ingestion or breathing in the poison are the most common ways a parakeet can become poisoned. Aerosol sprays and other products that leave a fine mist in the air can be particularly harmful for your little bird. Scented candles and plug-in air fresheners may seem harmless, but they can actually cause your parakeet respiratory distress or even death. Even candle "beads" that are unlit can seem like tasty pellets to your parakeet, and they can be deadly when ingested. Things like fertilizers, cleansers, and toxic houseplants are deadly, too. Keep your bird away from *all* household products.

Symptoms of poisoning can include vomiting, paralysis, bleeding from the eyes, nose, mouth, or vent, seizures, and shock.

MAKING A HOSPITAL CAGE

If your parakeet becomes injured or ill, put the bird in a safe, warm spot where it can't hurt itself further and where it can retain its body temperature, like a hospital cage, especially if you can't get your bird to your avian veterinarian right away. Making a hospital cage is easy. You'll need a 10-gallon aquarium or similarly sized plastic small animal tote, an aquarium thermometer, a heating pad, a screen top for the aquarium (or the plastic top that comes with the plastic animal tote, provided there are breathing holes), paper towels, and a small, rolled up washcloth.

Put the heating pad on the medium setting and place it underneath one half of the aquarium. Place a few layers of paper towels on the bottom of the aquarium, along with the rolled up washcloth as a soft perch. Put shallow dishes of food and water in the aquarium, and make sure the water is very shallow, because a weak bird can drown in water as deep as one inch. Place the bird in the aquarium; then cover the aquarium with the top and cover the aquarium three-fourths of the way with a dark towel. The bird should be able to move away from the heat if it wants to. Make sure that the temperature in the tank stays at about 90° F (about 32° C). You can also use a commercially designed snuggle up heater designed specifically for birds.

If you suspect that your bird has been poisoned, try an animal poison control hotline. The ASPCA Animal Poison Control Hotline can be reached 24/7/365 at 888-426-4435. Additionally, the Animal Poison Control Hotline is available 24/7/365 at 855-764-7661. Both charge a consultation fee.

If you can, rushing your parakeet to your avian veterinarian is essential to saving your bird's life, though quick response from you with the help of an animal poison control hotline can be crucial. For example, they may talk you through irrigating your bird's eyes or tell you whether or not what your bird ate is an issue or not. When in doubt, call.

Overheating

WARNING

If your parakeet is panting, holding its wings out, standing on two feet, or is even lying on the floor of the cage, it may be overcome with heat.

TIP

Keep a spray bottle handy and lightly mist your parakeet with cool water, repeating until it's soaked. Watch the bird closely until its behavior seems normal again. Make sure that your bird has cool water to drink at all times.

REMEMBER

Parakeets should never be kept in full sunlight unless they can retreat to a shady spot.

If your bird does not respond to misting, remove it from the spot immediately and place it in a cooler environment. If you have a small fan, place the flow of air so that it hits just beside the cage, not directly on it, and mist the bird again. Put drops of cool water in its beak if it's unable to drink. Call your avian veterinarian immediately.

Oil on the feathers

Oil on the feathers makes it difficult for a parakeet to regulate its body temperature, which can be deadly for a bird. The parakeet may also preen its feathers and ingest this oil, leading to medical problems. How does a parakeet get oil on its feathers? Believe it or not, parakeets occasionally fly into a pot of oil (cool oil, you hope!) or may even find themselves in the middle of an oily salad.

If your bird soaks itself in oil and is otherwise uninjured (the oil was cool), dust it with cornstarch or flour (any kind except gritty corn flour), making sure to keep the flour away from its face. Remove the excess flour with a paper towel. Fill a small tub with warm water and add some grease-fighting liquid dish soap. Gently place the bird in the tub and allow it to soak. You may have to repeat this a few times. Do not scrub! Rinse it using the same method (without the soap), blot it dry, and place the bird in a hospital cage with a heating pad underneath half of it and most of the top covered. Don't restrict the flow of air, but keep the heat in. Use a thermometer and make sure the cage is between 80° and 90° F (26° and 32° C). Then take your bird to your avian veterinarian.

Frostbite

Frostbite can cause the loss of toes and feet and may even result in death. If you keep your parakeet outdoors during the cold season, consider bringing it inside or add a safe heater as a preventative on the coldest nights. A parakeet will hold a frostbitten foot as if it were fractured (frostbite is a painful condition). The frostbitten area will die and turn a dark color.

If you find the condition early, place your bird in a hospital cage and slowly warm it to about 90° F (32° C) temperature and call the veterinarian. Monitor the bird to make sure that it is comfortable at all times and through the warming up process. If you catch the condition at the point where the affected area has already turned dark, get your bird to the avian veterinarian right away.

Unconsciousness

A bird may become unconscious for many reasons, but one strong possibility is that something is poisoning the air. If you find your bird unconscious, ventilate the room thoroughly and remove the bird from the area. Call your avian veterinarian immediately. If you're sure that there is no problem in the air, you can try to rouse your parakeet by gently handling the bird and trying to wake it. Get to your avian veterinarian right away.

Egg binding

A swollen abdomen may be a sign of egg binding in a female parakeet. If a hen is not well nourished, especially if she hasn't gotten enough calcium in her diet, her eggs may have soft shells, which will make the eggs difficult to lay, resulting in egg binding. Egg binding can also occur when the egg is malformed, or when the bird has a tumor or other disorder of the reproductive system. Symptoms of egg binding include panting and lameness. Consult your veterinarian immediately if you suspect this problem.

TIP

Normally, an egg is passed within a day of noticeable swelling. You will also notice large, patty-like stools. If you notice that your hen is having serious troubles and it's the middle of the night or you can't get to your avian veterinarian right away, move her to a warm (85° F to 90° F, or 29° C to 32° C) and humid hospital cage (see the sidebar earlier in this chapter for tips on making such a cage — to keep the humidity high, you can add a small, damp, rolled up washcloth). Gently place a few drops of mineral oil or olive oil in her beak with an eye dropper and place a few drops of the same in her vent (where the egg comes out), being extremely careful not to crush the egg. This may help her to pass the egg.

REMEMBER

Even if she does pass the egg, take her to the veterinarian as soon as you can.

Foot injuries

Don't try to correct a serious foot injury. Place the injured bird in a hospital cage and take it to the vet immediately. Most birds can live with missing toes and even missing feet if they are flighted and allowed to fly in a large space.

Eye injuries

If your parakeet's eye has come in contact with an irritant or poison, wash the eye out with saline solution before you take it to the veterinarian.

Sometimes parakeets can suffer eye injuries from thrashing around in the cage, being injured by another pet or predatory animal, or fighting with other birds in the cage or aviary. If the injury is from an animal bite or any other type of wound, place the bird in a hospital cage until you can get it to the veterinarian.

Seizures

A bird having seizures is in serious condition. Place it in a hospital cage and get to the veterinarian right away. If your parakeet comes out of the seizure, you may want to give it a few drops of sugar water (one teaspoon of sugar dissolved in 1 cup of water) to raise the blood sugar level and prevent a second seizure from occurring while on the way to the animal hospital.

Injury to the beak

Often, injuries to the beak can be fixed by a veterinarian, or the beak will heal itself by growing back. If your parakeet has injured its beak, place the bird in a hospital cage and take it to see the vet. Do not try to fix a beak problem yourself. (See Figure 9-2.)

FIGURE 9-2:
This parakeet's cracked beak should be seen by an avian veterinarian.

Chapter **10**

Bouncing Baby Budgies: Breeding Your Parakeets

I f you have two or more parakeets, you may want to breed them. But breeding parakeets isn't a matter of sticking two birds together and then waiting for the babies to arrive. You'd be surprised at how much parenting *you* actually have to do.

To Breed or Not to Breed?

Most parakeet enthusiasts recommend you don't breed your birds for a variety of reasons. However, people will freely do what they choose, so I want to make sure that you have all the knowledge you need to get started. Also, you might someday find yourself with a surprise clutch of babies, and this chapter will help you know what to do.

Before you even *consider* breeding your parakeets, keep in mind the following:

>> **Are you prepared for the extra expenses you will incur while breeding your parakeets?** Expenses include the cost of equipment, potential veterinary visits, formula, and housing for the youngsters, among many others.

>> **Are your birds in perfect health?** How do you know? When was the last time they had a regular checkup at your avian veterinarian? If you breed birds who aren't in perfect health, you run the risk of ending up with offspring who — you guessed it — aren't in perfect health, and you also put the parents' health at great risk as well. Breeding birds need to direct all their strength and energy toward the demanding tasks of egg laying, incubation, hatching, and raising young, rather than having to fight off illness and disease.

>> **Do you have a regular avian veterinarian or birdy mentor who will take your calls at all hours when something goes wrong with the parents or the babies?** Raising baby birds isn't easy; you'll need access to an experienced, qualified expert 24/7.

>> **Are you able to handle the fact that you may lose one or more of your parent parakeets or babies to breeding complications?** Watching a baby bird die isn't easy, but it's often a fact of life.

>> **Will you care when your previously tame parakeets become nippy and territorial?** When your birds have babies, their focus is no longer on being your companion; instead they will shift to protecting and raising their young.

>> **Do you have the time and the know-how to hand-feed the young if the parents reject them?** Birds, especially young parents, do sometimes reject their babies, and if that happens, you'll have to care for the young'uns until they are weaned and eating on their own.

>> **Can you handle giving away or selling your precious babies?** Unless you have the room for a large flock of birds, you'll need to find a home for each of the babies — and not just *any* home, but a good home.

>> **Are you prepared to keep all the babies if you can't find homes for them or they turn out physically challenged in some way?** When you bring new babies into the world, you're responsible for caring for them, and if you can't find a home for all your babies, you'll have to keep them yourself.

These questions are only some of the things you'll have to consider when you embark on parakeet husbandry. Often, it's more trouble than it's worth. On the other hand, after you gain some experience, it can be a fun and rewarding hobby, especially if your goal is to breed English budgies for show purposes.

TIP

Parakeets can physically breed at six months of age, but you should wait until your pair is at least a year old and in prime breeding condition because they will be much more likely to be successful at feeding and raising their own young when they are bred at the proper breeding age.

Preventing Breeding

REMEMBER

If you *don't* want your pair to breed, simply don't offer them anything nest-like, such as a dark, cozy place to sleep, like a box or a bird hut. They'll be fine sleeping on a perch. If they insist on breeding anyway and are nesting on the bottom of the cage or in the seed dish, they may be getting too many hours of light. Cut back their light to ten hours a day, and cut out any soft or wet foods that could substitute for young seeds that are found during the breeding season in their natural habitat. Continue to supplement their diet with dark green leafy vegetables and red, orange, and yellow vegetables. This approach should calm their hormones a bit, but it may not prevent them from trying to nest in a food dish or at the bottom of the cage.

Some hens won't stop laying eggs no matter what you do, even if there isn't a male around to be the daddy. This is a problem because the bird can succumb to malnutrition and calcium deficiency. If you remove the eggs, the hen may just keep laying. You can try allowing your hen to continue to sit on the infertile eggs for up to a month, when she is more likely to abandon them naturally on her own accord. This may give her the feeling that she has completed her task.

Conditioning Your Parent Parakeets

Wild parakeets breed only when food is bountiful in the spring and summer. Captive parakeets have bountiful food all the time, so they will breed any time of year.

Your birds have to be in top shape to be able to successfully rear young without incident. You have to feed them well before you attempt to breed them, which means they must eat plenty of fresh fruits and veggies and egg food, which will give them the protein they require. You must also offer them a good source of calcium, such as a cuttle bone, well-cooked eggshells, and calcium powder in their soft food so that your hen has enough to create the eggshells without leeching too much calcium from her bones.

Your parent birds also need a lot of exercise, which means they need a large space where they can fly.

Your hen will also need a lot of fresh water when she's creating eggs. Staying hydrated helps her lay the eggs without issue.

Breeding Equipment

If you want to breed your parakeets, you'll need the proper nest. Wild parakeets nest in holes in trees. In captivity, most guardians offer their parakeets a wooden nest box. You can find them online or in most pet stores. Here's what you'll need:

>> **The nest box:** The breeding box will have a shallow concave area where the eggs will rest. Add a small handful of soft shavings for the parents to arrange to their liking.

Adding some pine shavings helps to keep the nest clean as babies excrete their droppings into the litter and ensure that the babies don't get splay leg, which is a condition that's difficult to correct.

>> **The incubator:** You will also need an incubator. These are available online or at most farm equipment stores. Why would you need an incubator when you're going to let the parents sit on the eggs and raise the babies? Because sometimes the parents kick out the eggs and babies, or abandon them, or are aggressive toward them, scrambling the eggs and harming the babies. In these cases, you will have to take over, and you'll need a safe place to keep the eggs and babies in the proper temperature and humidity.

>> **A cage for the fledglings:** You will need a separate flight cage to house the babies after they wean at about six to seven weeks of age. You can't keep them with their parents, or the adults will attack them to drive them from the nest, especially if they parents have gone back to nest. Also, be careful that the babies don't mature around each other and start breeding. This does happen!

>> **Leg bands:** Finally, you will need closed leg bands to slip onto the babies' legs when they are around 8 days old to identify them. You can order bands from The American Budgerigar Society at https://abs1.org/orderbands/ or from L&M Let Bands at http://w.1mbirdlegbands.com.

Setting up for Breeding

Parakeets are happy to breed in a flock situation in an aviary as long as there's enough space and you only include true, bonded pairs. Make sure that you have no fewer than three pairs (six birds: three male, three female). Offer at least four or five nest boxes so that they have choices. Place the nest boxes in an area that will stay dry in inclement weather and place them as high in the aviary as you can, but with enough space that the birds can perch on the top of the nest. (See Figure 10-1.)

FIGURE 10-1: These parakeets are nesting communally in a breeding colony.

Realize that if you toss an equivalent number of males and females and allow them to pair up as they choose, you won't be able to control the genetics of the babies. This may not matter to you. Most parakeet enthusiast breeders intentionally set up individual pairs, one pair per cage, that they believe will produce specific color mutations. If you don't care about coloration, you can allow your birds to choose their own mates.

If you have just one or two pairs, you can breed them in their normal cages or transfer them to flight cages (each pair by itself) where they can get the exercise they need to remain in good condition as they nest and raise young.

WARNING

If you put a male and a female together and they aren't cuddling and preening each other, you'll have to try another pairing. With most parrots, pairing is love at first sight. (See Figure 10-2.) They generally don't fall in love gradually. An unmatched pair can even become aggressive with each other, so don't push them to match up.

If you are breeding one pair per cage, you can hang the nest box outside the cage, which will allow you to peek inside the box to see what's going on, or you can hang the box inside the cage, but it will be more difficult to open the boxes and intervene if something goes wrong.

Waiting Game: The Breeding Timeline

When you have a true pair (a cock and a hen) that are in love and in good breeding condition, and you've added a nest to their housing, it's only a matter of time before you have some chicks. Here's the basic breeding timeline:

>> The pair will cuddle and preen each other, and the male will feed the female by regurgitating his food to her.

>> They will enter the nest and go back and forth out of it. Sometimes the male will have to coax the female into the nest if she's tentative.

>> You may notice the pair mating; the male will stand of top of the female, then swing sideways with one wing out-stretched to hold the female, while rubbing their cloacas together.

>> After mating, the hen will usually lay her first egg in eight to ten days. You may notice that her droppings have become larger and patty-like. She may also breathe heavily as she's getting ready to lay the egg and her abdomen will be swollen. She is eggnant!

>> She will then lay an egg every other day until she has laid five to seven eggs.

>> After she lays her last egg, she will start sitting on the clutch of eggs and the male will come feed her. (See Figure 10-3.)

>> Around 18 to 22 days after she has begun sitting on her eggs, the first egg should hatch. They will hopefully hatch out about every other day. You may be tempted to check the nest box a lot — it's exciting! But refrain from checking too often, if you can, especially with new parents. Check very quickly about twice a day when you notice that the hen has left the nest to eat or bathe.

>> If conditions for keeping her young alive aren't ideal, or if she's not being fed well or isn't feeling well, she may abandon, pluck, or even kill the babies. This is why you must keep your birds in exceptional condition and check on the babies occasionally.

>> Ten to fourteen days after hatching, you will notice feathers starting to grow on the babies.

>> When their eyes open, you can temporarily block the nest box hole so that the parents can't enter, and then handle the babies. If you do this every day, they will get used to human touch. Make these visits brief or stop if the visits stress the parents prompting them to quit feeding, abandon, or harm the young.

FIGURE 10-3: This female parakeet keeps her babies warm.

>> About 28 days after they are hatched, the chicks are now fully feathered fledglings and they will start to spend time out of the nest. Offer soft foods and water to encourage them to eat and drink on their own.

>> At six weeks of age (42 days), the babies are now fully flighted and must be moved to another cage or risk being attacked by the parents. This also allows the parents some needed rest.

Handfeeding Baby Parakeets

Sometimes you may have to intervene and handfeed your baby parakeets. New parents can be neglectful or even hurt the babies, so you've got to be prepared. I strongly recommend having a birdy mentor help you learn this process.

TIP

If you want to pull the babies from the nest to handfeed because you want them to be super friendly, pull them at about two weeks, or just after their eyes have opened. You want them to have seen and acknowledged their birdy parents before you take over. They will actually be friendlier in the long run if you do it this way.

TIP

There are several brands of commercially produced handfeeding formula, making your job a lot easier. Follow the instructions on the packaging.

Handfeeding isn't difficult, but there are pitfalls. Here are a few issues to avoid:

>> **Aspirating a baby:** This is when the food goes down the windpipe instead of the esophagus and the baby chokes to death. It can happen very fast.

>> **Ovefeeding:** If you feed too much at one time, the crop (the sac on the chest where the food goes) can expand too much, creating spaces for bacteria to thrive, and can also damage the muscles in the crop.

>> **Feeding when the baby isn't ready:** Only feed a baby that has an empty crop. It's healthy for them to completely digest their food and be begging for a feeding before you feed again. Don't try to feed a baby that isn't showing a feeding response.

>> **Overheating:** Feeding baby formula that's too hot can cause crop burn, which is fatal in a bird this small. Stir the formula well to eliminate any hot spots at the center and use a thermometer to ensure that the formula is no warmer than between 104 and 106 degrees Fahrenheit (40 and 41.11 degrees Celsius). Higher temperatures can scald the crop causing crop burn.

>> **Underheating:** Cold baby formula can cause crop slow-down, which can also be deadly.

>> **Old formula:** Formula must be made fresh every single time you feed. I can't stress this enough. You can't put the formula in the refrigerator and take it out each time you feed. Bacteria can grow in the old formula and kill your babies.

If you are handfeeding very young chicks that are still naked and whose eyes aren't open, you have to keep them warm or their food will not digest. You can use an incubator, a brooder, or you can use a plastic small animal keeper (with a top) and set it partially on top of a heating pad. Line the bottom with paper towels and pine shavings and be sure to clean it each time you feed the babies.

Keep the temperature at about 98 degrees Fahrenheit (36.6 Celsius) for young chicks without feathers and lower it gradually to 85 degrees Fahrenheit (29.4 Celsius) when they start growing feathers. After the feathers have come in, you can lower the temperature to 70 degrees Fahrenheit (21.11 Celsius) or a comfortable room temperature. Babies should adapt to room temperature before transferring them to their own cage. Move the babies to a cage when all of their feathers have grown in and they have begun to eat by themselves.

Babies between one day and five days old need to be fed around the clock, about every two hours, and the formula should be thin – you will thicken the formula as the baby get solder. At first, you only need a drop or two of formula per feeding. As the chicks get older, feedings can become less frequent, feeding only when the crop is empty. Chicks older than one week of age can be fed once during the night, and as the babies grow they should be able to go through the night until early morning, but they shouldn't go more than seven or eight hours overnight without a feeding.

Babies grow at their own pace. Table 10-1 offers a guide to feeding, but it's just a guide. You may have to do more feedings or feed for longer. It's important that the chicks completely digest all of their food before you offer another feeding, but never let them go without food for too long.

TABLE 10-1   **Feeding Chart**

Age of Chicks	Feeding Rate
1 to 5 days	Feed every 2 hours around the clock.
6 to 7 days	Feedings at 7 am, 11 am, 3 pm, 7 pm, and 11 pm, and one middle of the night feeding (you can vary the times, but keep to every 3 or 4 hours).
8 to 14 days	Same as for chicks at 6 to 7 days of age, but eliminate the middle of the night feeding.
15 to 30 days	Feed 4 to 5 times daily, when the chicks are hungry and the crop is full.
31 to 35 days	Feed 3 to 4 times a day when the chicks are hungry. Start introducing millet spray and soft foods for the chicks to explore.
36 to 42 days	Feed 2 to 3 times a day. Offer millet spray and soft foods to encourage the chicks to eat on their own.
42 days and older	Feed 1 to 2 times a day until weaned.

You can begin feeding very young chicks with a small pipette or thin syringe without a needle tip. Heat the formula in the microwave and stir it *very* well to avoid hot spots. Test the formula on the inside of your wrist and/or with a thermometer. If it's too hot, allow it to cool.

Pull some of the formula into the syringe and then push it a little to let the air out. Next, place the syringe on the baby's beak and squeeze a very small amount onto it. The baby should instinctively gobble the small amount formula.

WARNING

Never force the syringe into the beak or try to feed too much. Let the baby do the work. Feeding is over once you notice that the crop is full (it will look like a bubble on the baby's chest), but not so full that it's taut or overly full; the formula should never be seen above the Adam's apple or the baby could aspirate.

REMEMBER

Make sure to wipe the baby's beak so that the formula doesn't dry or become caked on its face or it could lead to a deformed beak. Keeping the babies clean is very important. Also, clean and disinfect your feeding tools very well after each feeding.

When the babies are a little older, it's easy to feed them safely using a spoon that has been bent on its sides to create kind of a funnel. You can find these online, and there are even bent spoons that attach to a syringe.

Weaning the Babies

The babies will be ready to start exploring solid food when they are at about three feedings a day, or about four to five weeks of age. Give them millet spray, egg food, brown rice, dark green leafy vegetables, and shallow bowls of pellets. A week after that, you can start incorporating some fresh veggies. Chop them into small bites to make them easy to eat, and offer them both cooked and warm and cold.

When they are feathered out and eating a little on their own, you can put them into a cage with some low perches to get them used to climbing and perching. Add some toys for enrichment and entertainment.

Keep handfeeding the babies, even if you see that they are eating solid food. They should be eating by themselves at six to eight weeks, but some are late bloomers and will still want to be handfed. This is normal. It's better to handfeed a little longer than risk starving your babies. Although parent-raised parakeets wean by 42 days of age, it is not that unusual for handfed babies to take longer when they are being foster-fed by people.

TIP

If you have a baby that's still begging for food when the rest of its clutch mates are already weaned, keep handfeeding that baby until it catches up. Don't starve the babies in an effort to wean them faster. They will wean when they are ready. Send a baby to its new home only when it is completely weaned and off of hand-feeding formula and it has a full, round crop at night at least several nights in a row. This way you will know that it's eating plenty on its own.

The Part
of Tens

Chapter **11**

Ten Facts about Parakeets

>> **A female parakeet usually lays four to six eggs per clutch (a *clutch* is a group of eggs and then babies when they hatch) but can lay as many as eight to ten eggs, with five to seven eggs being the average clutch size.** It takes the eggs 18 to 20 days to hatch.

>> **Parakeets can learn to talk as early as 3 months of age.** Both males and females can learn to talk and whistle.

>> **Parakeets have been recorded speaking 600 to 800 words!** Other parrots, even good talkers, may learn half of that or far less. Some larger parrots may learn only a few words or not talk at all.

>> **When a parakeet bites, it's usually because the bird is afraid or defending its territory or its mate.** But it could also be defending a toy or something else it's attached to. Most of the time, it's biting because you're trying to catch or restrain him.

>> **Parakeets can't be *hybridized*, or crossed, with another type of bird.** Other parrots, like conures or macaws, can breed and produce offspring with another parrot in their own genus.

>> **The average parakeet can live 8 years or longer if taken care of properly.** Most parakeets will live to be far less, but you can extend the lifespan of your bird with good nutrition and exercise.

>> **In the wild, parakeets often flock in large numbers.** They've been seen in flocks of more than 20,000 to 30,000 birds.

>> **Myth has it that *albino* parakeets (which are white with red eyes) are blind — but this is not the case.** Albinos can see as well as their pigmented cousins.

>> **The *crested parakeet* is a mutation of the normally feathered parakeet.** It has a Beatles' Ringo Starr mop "hairdo" on top of its head. Very cute!

>> **Parakeets like company.** They can be kept peaceably in a large aviary with zebra finches, cockatiels, and Bourke's parakeets, all of which are also from Australia. If the budgies are in pairs, keep an eye on the other species to be certain they are not being bullied by the parakeets.

Chapter **12**

Ten Fun and Informative Parakeet and Budgie Websites

>> **American Budgerigar Society** (www.abs1.org): This is a great source of information about keeping, breeding, and exhibiting parakeets.

>> **Budgerigar Association of America** (www.budgerigaras sociation.com): This is the website of the publisher of *Budgerigar Journal Magazine*.

>> **World Budgerigar Organization** (https://www.world-budgerigar.org): This organization supports and encourages the free movement of budgerigar breeders and budgerigars across international borders in order to improve the breeding, exhibiting, and judging of budgerigars.

- **Mort's Budgie World** (https://www.mortsbudgieworld.com): Exhibition budgie breeder in Australia. Lots of good information about genetics and show budgies.

- **Budgie Info** (https://www.budgie-info.com): This site contains a wealth of information about parakeet and budgie care and breeding.

- **Omlet** (https://www.omlet.co.uk/guide/budgies): This general pet website has dozens of pages dedicated to budgies with information ranging from general care to training.

- **The Budgerigar Society** (https://www.budgerigarsociety.com): This site is dedicated to showing budgies in the UK.

- **Budgie World** (www.budgieworld.org): This budgie fan site offers lots of great information about budgies and includes a budgie wiki.

- **Tri-State Budgerigar Society** (http://www.tri-statebudgie.org/index.html): Offers information on showing and show calendars.

- **Facebook. Search for the following groups:**
  - Budgies101
  - Budgie Addicts Support Group
  - Budgie Group
  - Budgies: Help and Advice
  - Budgie Lovers
  - Budgie Planet Group
  - Budgie Whisperers
  - Parakeets (the largest parakeet group on Facebook)
  - Parakeet Pro: Help and Advice Regarding Your Budgies
  - Toy Making for Budgies and Parrots
  - Budgies & English Budgies
  - Budgerigar Expert Chatroom and Pictures

  . . . and *many* more!

Index

F

fear, in parakeets, 92–93

feather plucking, 93

feathers
  blood, 81, 84
  checking health of parakeets with, 119–120
  contour, 76
  down, 76
  examining, 36
  flight, 76
  fluffing, 88
  oiled, 127–128
  pin, 81, 82, 84, 120
  primary, 11
  secondary, 11
  shaking, 88
  on tail, 76

feeding chart, 141

feeding parakeets
  cooked foods, 68–69
  dietary requirements, 63–64
  foods to avoid, 69–70
  fresh water, 62
  fruits and vegetables, 65–67
  nutritional supplements, 70–71
  overview, 61
  pellets, 65
  recipes for, 70–74
  seeds, 64–65
  snacks, 67–68
  table foods, 68–69

feet
  checking health of parakeets, 36
  description of, 11
  examining, 119
  injuries to, 129

female parakeets, selecting for purchase, 30–31

filoplumes, 76

flapping wings, 90

flat perches, 45

flea markets, purchasing parakeets from, 33

fledglings
  cages for, 135
  handfeeding, 139–142
  selecting for purchase, 28–29
  weaning, 139–142

flight cages, 38–39

flight feathers, 76

fluffing feathers, 88

food
  cooked foods, 68–69
  dietary requirements, 63–64
  foods to avoid, 69–70
  fresh water, 62
  fruits and vegetables, 65–67
  nutritional supplements, 70–71
  overview, 61
  pellets, 65
  recipes, 70–74
  replacing old, 16
  seeds, 64–65
  snacks, 67–68
  table foods, 68–69

formula, 140–142, 143

fresh water, checking for, 62

frostbite, 128

fruits, 65–67

full flight, 36

G

gifting parakeets, 25

gizzard, 71

grinding beaks, 87

grit, 71

grooming
  bathing, 77–78
  overview, 75
  preening, 75–77
  toenail clipping, 76
  wing clipping, 78–82

H

habitats, 38–39

handfeeding, 139–142

About the Author

Nikki Moustaki, M.A., M.F.A., is an avian care and behavior consultant and the author more than 30 books on birds and bird behavior. She is also the author of the bird-related memoir, *The Bird Market of Paris.* She has kept and/or bred lovebirds, cockatiels, budgies (parakeets), lories, macaws, amazons, conures, finches, canaries, ringnecks, and brotergeris. She advocates for responsible bird care and encourages everyone to participate in avian rescue efforts.

Dedication

You have no idea how high I can fly.

Author's Acknowledgments

I would like to thank everyone who made this book possible, including Kelsey Baird, Christopher Morris, Michelle Hacker, Siddique Shaik, and Linda S. Rubin.

Publisher's Acknowledgments

Acquisitions Editor: Kelsey Baird

Project Editor: Christopher Morris

Copy Editor: Christopher Morris

Technical Editor: Linda S. Rubin

Production Editor:
Vivek Lakshmikanth

Cover Image: © Khmel/iStock/ Getty Images

Take dummies with you everywhere you go!

Whether you are excited about e-books, want more from the web, must have your mobile apps, or are swept up in social media, dummies makes everything easier.

Find us online!

dummies.com

dummies
A Wiley Brand

Leverage the power

Dummies is the global leader in the reference category and one of the most trusted and highly regarded brands in the world. No longer just focused on books, customers now have access to the dummies content they need in the format they want. Together we'll craft a solution that engages your customers, stands out from the competition, and helps you meet your goals.

Advertising & Sponsorships

Connect with an engaged audience on a powerful multimedia site, and position your message alongside expert how-to content. Dummies.com is a one-stop shop for free, online information and know-how curated by a team of experts.

- Targeted ads
- Video
- Email Marketing
- Microsites
- Sweepstakes sponsorship

20 **MILLION**
PAGE VIEWS
EVERY SINGLE MONTH

15 MILLION **UNIQUE**
VISITORS PER MONTH

43%
OF ALL VISITORS
ACCESS THE SITE
VIA THEIR MOBILE DEVICES

700,000 NEWSLETTE
SUBSCRIPTIO
TO THE INBOXES OF
300,000 UNIQUE INDIVIDUALS
EVERY WEEK

# of dummies

Custom Publishing

Reach a global audience in any language by creating a solution that will differentiate you from competitors, amplify your message, and encourage customers to make a buying decision.

- Apps
- Books
- eBooks
- Video
- Audio
- Webinars

Brand Licensing & Content

Leverage the strength of the world's most popular reference brand to reach new audiences and channels of distribution.

For more information, visit **dummies.com/biz**

PERSONAL ENRICHMENT

Staying Sharp
9781119187790
USA $26.00
CAN $31.99
UK £19.99

Facebook
9781119179030
USA $21.99
CAN $25.99
UK £16.99

Guitar
9781119293354
USA $24.99
CAN $29.99
UK £17.99

Investing
9781119293347
USA $22.99
CAN $27.99
UK £16.99

Beekeeping
9781119310068
USA $22.99
CAN $27.99
UK £16.99

Digital Photography
9781119235606
USA $24.99
CAN $29.99
UK £17.99

Meditation
9781119251163
USA $24.99
CAN $29.99
UK £17.99

Pregnancy
9781119235491
USA $26.99
CAN $31.99
UK £19.99

Samsung Galaxy S7
9781119279952
USA $24.99
CAN $29.99
UK £17.99

iPhone
9781119283133
USA $24.99
CAN $29.99
UK £17.99

Crocheting
9781119287117
USA $24.99
CAN $29.99
UK £16.99

Nutrition
9781119130246
USA $22.99
CAN $27.99
UK £16.99

PROFESSIONAL DEVELOPMENT

Windows 10
9781119311041
USA $24.99
CAN $29.99
UK £17.99

AutoCAD
9781119255796
USA $39.99
CAN $47.99
UK £27.99

Excel 2016
9781119293439
USA $26.99
CAN $31.99
UK £19.99

QuickBooks 2017
9781119281467
USA $26.99
CAN $31.99
UK £19.99

macOS Sierra
9781119280651
USA $29.99
CAN $35.99
UK £21.99

LinkedIn
9781119251132
USA $24.99
CAN $29.99
UK £17.99

Windows 10
9781119310563
USA $34.00
CAN $41.99
UK £24.99

SharePoint 2016
9781119181705
USA $29.99
CAN $35.99
UK £21.99

Fundamental Analysis
9781119263593
USA $26.99
CAN $31.99
UK £19.99

Networking
9781119257769
USA $29.99
CAN $35.99
UK £21.99

Office 2016
9781119293477
USA $26.99
CAN $31.99
UK £19.99

Office 365
9781119265313
USA $24.99
CAN $29.99
UK £17.99

Salesforce.com
9781119239314
USA $29.99
CAN $35.99
UK £21.99

Coding
9781119293323
USA $29.99
CAN $35.99
UK £21.99

dummies.com

dummies
A Wiley Brand

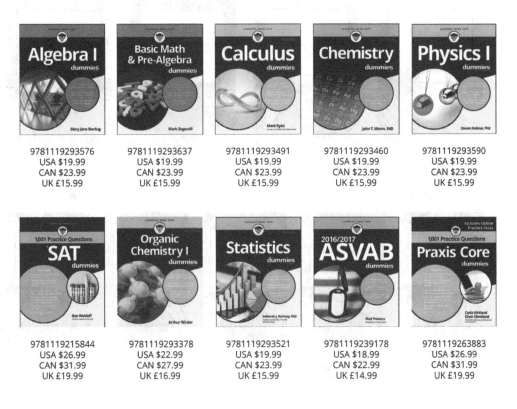

Small books for big imaginations

Unleash Their Creativity

dummies.com